The Old Money Guide to Marriage

GETTING IT RIGHT & MAKING IT LAST

BYRON TULLY

Copyright © 2015 by Byron Tully

Cover Photo Credit: Weatherford Bradley. All rights reserved.

All rights reserved. No part of this book may be used or reproduced by any means, graphic, electronic, or mechanical, including photocopying, recording, taping, or by any information storage retrieval system, without the written permission of the publisher except in the case of brief quotations embodied in critical articles and reviews.

ISBN: 978-1-950118-08-3 (paperback), 978-1-950118-06-9 (hardback)

FRIDAY, FEBRUARY 14, 1964, PASADENA, TEXAS

BE MY VALENTINE --- Says Byron Tully, 817 Mobile, to Barbara Houston, 517 Center. The two children are students at Miss Marie's Private School, 302 S. Randall.

Contents

Introduction 1
The Stages Of Life 9
Your Childhood Experience 17
Your Education Experience 23
Your Friends And Family 29
Your Social Class 37
Your Values 45
Your Dating Experience 53
Your First Commitment—Exclusivity 63
Your Second Commitment—Engagement 69
Your Biggest Commitment—Marriage 79
Your Expectations 89
Your Mutual Understandings 93
Your Household 99
Your Finances 103
Your Health 113
Your Social Circle 117
Your Work 121
Your In-Laws And Extended Family 127
Your Personal Growth 133
Children 139
In Their Own Words 151
In Summary 157
About the Author 161

Introduction

First, let me acknowledge that there are thousands of educated and highly-qualified professionals who have committed their lives to helping individuals and couples improve, repair, and nourish their relationships within the institution of marriage.

Many of them may be more qualified than I am, in terms of credentials and experience, to comment and advise on the subject of being happily married. Furthermore, thousands of books are published every year on the subject, some with more merit than others. Some, let's be honest, are simply blatant commercial ventures by publishing companies or ego trips by authors with very little value to offer anyone, married or not. Some offer valid and helpful insights and, many times, justifiably become popular and well-regarded.

In light of these facts, I would present this book as a single resource among many. The opinions presented in it belong solely to me. Feel free to disagree or disregard. I would encourage you to take your time and weigh the concepts presented before you accept them straightaway or dismiss them as bunk. Odds are that you, the reader, have not been happily married to the same person for over a quarter of a century. I have. That fact alone should warrant a measure of consideration. There is also the assumption that, if you are reading this book, you want to have an enduring and joyful marriage with someone. I admire and respect that aspiration. I want to contribute to your success in that endeavor.

My experience in married life, coupled with my experience in the culture of Old Money in America, which was articulated in "The Old Money Book", provides the basis and perspective for this book. I discussed marriage to a certain extent in "The Old Money Book". As copies sold, I received correspondence from many people about their personal relationships. Most often, it was a question about a person that they were considering marrying.

Those inquiries became the motivation for this book. To be clear, I approach marriage as someone who holds and promotes traditional values. I think a person should be honest, honor their commitments, have integrity, be loyal, have a code of behavior that they live by, be kind to everyone as much as possible (especially their loved ones), be polite, and stand up for things they believe in. I think being dogmatic is dangerous, but that being wishy-washy or conveniently flexible about important things in life is even more dangerous.

The traditional values I hold dear and live my life by are not euphemisms for racism, homophobia, or elitism. Socioeconomic level, language, culture, skin color, religion, sexual preference — these differences are superficial in nature. I'm telling you this as someone who routinely sits in restaurants and cafes and listens to conversations between all kinds of couples: gay, straight, Muslim, Christian. Couples in khakis and penny loafers, couples with tattoos, piercings, and florescent hair, couples who share each other's mascara and even wear each other's clothes…I see it all and don't judge any of it.

Why? Because, first, it's not my place to judge it, and second, because their conversations sound so very much the same. They're trying to figure out where they're going to live, who they're going to invite to their wedding, what's going on with their job, what they're going to do about their children, how they're going to take care of an aging parent. They're in the business of marriage, or they're about to be in it. Their situations and their appearances vary. Their challenges are universal. (I tell you this sincerely: you have not been truly amused until you hear a reputation-heavy rock star complain about a young man his daughter is dating.)

The values couples often use to navigate these challenges are universal, too. These values, what I called Core Values in "The Old Money Book", are shared by most people the world over. They hold our countries, communities, and families together. They bring out the best in us, give us a sense of purpose and boundaries, of right and wrong, of fair play, and simply make the world a better place.

Marriage, and the family unit that often results from it, is an institution. It is also one of these values. My experience and observations about what makes a marriage work, what makes it joyful, and what makes it grow, are presented in this book. They may not be wholly original. I don't really care. They are time-tested and worthwhile. That is what is important to me.

But understand this: I am not preaching to you from an ivory tower or a mountaintop, all-wise and all-knowing. I am still married, still learning, still making mistakes, still being forgiven, and still forgiving. I'm also still laughing, still loving, and still grateful at the mystery and wonder of it all.

As the reader, you're making a couple of assumptions about me: that I know what I'm writing about and that I can articulate it clearly. As the writer, I'm making a couple of assumptions about you: that you have an open mind and that you believe in the institution of marriage. We both have to bring these things to the table or else our arrangement is not going to be satisfactory for very long.

If we've both articulated and agreed upon these assumptions, and we both agree to act honorably upon them, then there's a chance that you'll have the satisfaction of an enjoyable read, and you might learn something. I'll have the satisfaction of sharing what I know, and I might help someone.

This mutually beneficial, mutual satisfying arrangement between two parties who agree to perform in a certain way is a large part of what marriage is, ten times a day, for decades, between two imperfect human beings who are constantly growing, who have jobs and parents and friends and often children, in a turbulent world that is constantly changing and that is, many times, unfair.

Marriage is also a fountain of love, trust, devotion, and inspiration. It is an emotional fortress and sanctuary, unmatched in providing comfort, stability, laughter, and joy.

Marriage provides a proven and honorable way to share your life with someone, have and raise children with them, as well as create, preserve, and pass on wealth and wisdom to future generations. It's something you want to get right for numerous reasons. It's a huge contributor to happiness. It's a big factor in health. It provides a sense of purpose in life.

What's more, I'm not really sure if you can call someone 'successful' if they can't manage to be successfully married. To me, someone either lacks a general awareness about who they are and what they really need and want in a relationship, or there's a personal issue that someone is unwilling to correct. Of course, we all make mistakes. To be married in error once is understandable. To marry and divorce two or three times is indicative of a bigger issue, or several. It hints at a lack of judgment or an inability to follow through on a commitment.

Make no mistake: people do consider your track record in marriage in all sorts of decisions. Personally, I'm not going to let someone who can't manage their personal life manage my money. I want someone stable. I want someone with a sense of the long term. I want someone who's on an even keel.

As I did in "The Old Money Book", I'm going to offer two examples, Jill and Jane, who both start out dating and get married, but end up in two very different places in life years later. Each one meets someone and falls in love, but it's the choices they make at different stages in their relationships and their lives that make huge differences in their overall happiness.

Jill is a sophomore in college, majoring in business, and thinking about a career in commercial real estate. Her family is working class, and she aspires to a white-collar job and upward mobility. She meets Ray and feels an instant attraction for him. They begin to date and soon Jill has fallen in love. Ray is a senior in college and will graduate in the spring. He proposes to Jill and she accepts. They are both so much in love that they want to get married right away. Ray will be moving back home after graduation, and Jill decides to follow him. Jill's parents have money set aside for her to complete college, but after she pleads with them to let her use the money for her dream wedding, they agree and give their blessing. She will not graduate from college, but will instead follow Ray to his hometown and begin their life together there.

Jill meets Ray's parents shortly thereafter, and they all begin to plan the wedding. Ray graduates from college in the spring, and the summer wedding is a success, even though it ended up costing a little bit more than Jill and Ray expected. They leave the morning after and enjoy a wonderful honeymoon in an exotic location. Jill's dream has come true: she has met and married her Prince Charming and had the wedding she will always remember.

The two of them rent a small apartment in Ray's hometown, and he goes to work at a local trucking company. Jill also looks for a job and even considers going back to school to finish her degree, but their finances don't allow for that, as the money her parents had saved for college was spent on the wedding. Jill finds a part-time job that doesn't pay that well, as she's not a college graduate, and any career that she had planned for herself seems a very long way off for a moment. But she's in love, and they're together, and that's all that matters. (Whenever someone says, 'That's all that matters', it isn't.)

A few months later, Jill and Ray learn that they're expecting a baby. It's something Ray had always wanted and he's delighted. Jill is happy, too, but it means that the career that she thought she'd move into after marriage is now even farther in the distance. But she's going to be a mother, and that, too, was a dream of hers. When the baby is born, Jill quits her part-time job and is a full-time mother. She loves and adores her child. Ray is very happy. He has a steady job with a reliable paycheck at a job he enjoys. But life for Jill is becoming less of her dream and more of a reality.

The reality is that Ray is not very ambitious and is content to work at the trucking company for the rest of his career. He also wants more children. Jill had never really thought about these things when they were dating, so the subject of work, family, career, and where they both wanted to be in five years was never seriously discussed in detail.

To add to the stress, Jill feels trapped. She feels she doesn't have as much of a voice in their marriage as she would like because she isn't earning her own money to contribute to it. Jill and Ray work to address these issues, but, after a heated exchange, they both realize that they had very different expectations about what their lives would be like as a married couple.

They agree to try to work through it. They agree that Jill will go back to school at a local community college and finish her degree. Then she can pursue her career in commercial real estate as she planned. But a month later, Ray loses his job at the trucking company. He doesn't handle it well, and Jill sees a side of him that she'd never seen before. (They only dated for six months before getting married, so how could she know he wouldn't handle disappointment well?)

Ray begins to drink, doesn't look for work as diligently as he should, and financial pressures from the lack of income mount. Finally, Jill has had enough. Desperate and broke, she calls her parents and asks if she can come home with her baby. They welcome her home with open arms.

Now, she must face the challenges before her. She and Ray will divorce. His support, emotional and financial, will be inconsistent until he finds another job and addresses his own personal issues. She must care for her child and find work. Her parents are supportive, but she can't stay with them forever. Jill has a long road ahead of her, and she is not yet twenty-five years old.

Jane, too, is a sophomore in college. She meets Dan and feels an instant chemistry between them. Dan is also a senior and will graduate in the spring. Very soon after meeting each other, they decide to start seeing each other exclusively.

At the graduation ceremony for Dan, Jane introduces her parents to Dan's family. They all enjoy a celebratory dinner together. Both of the families learn that Dan and Jane have been dating each other exclusively for six months, and they want to continue that arrangement. Dan will be moving a short distance from Jane, as she remains on campus to finish her college education. They plan to see each other on weekends and holidays, with Dan coming into town or Jane visiting him in the city.

It's difficult not to be together as much as they would like, but Jane and Dan both agree that her staying in school is the best choice. Dan starts his new job in the city that summer, and Jane starts her junior year in college that fall. Each meet other people in social settings, but the spark just isn't the same.

During their first year apart, Dan's father dies unexpectedly. Jane comforts him, but she learns that, in seeing him face this difficult time, Dan needs a lot of time alone when he's feeling stressed. She fights her instinct to instantly want to fix things and ask how he's doing. Eventually, in his own time and his own way, he communicates with her. They go through a trying time together and grow closer because of it. Jane also becomes closer with Dan's mother. Jane and Dan continue to see each other, and the next summer Dan proposes to Jane during a vacation weekend that includes both families. Everyone is delighted.

Jane and Dan announce to their families that they've agreed on a two-year engagement. They've been dating each other exclusively, and have been practically engaged for almost two years, but they feel waiting another two years to get married will be worth it. Dan doesn't want to work at a job all his life, and going into business for himself will be a big move, so he needs to prepare for that. Jane wants to teach. She plans to get a job immediately after graduation. She and Dan have had long discussions about his desire to be in business for himself at some point in time. They have agreed that her steady salary as a teacher would be a great asset in helping him fulfill his dreams. She has also expressed her desire to live abroad at some point and take classes at Oxford. Dan has agreed that he'll arrange his business so that, when the opportunity arises, they can live abroad for a period of time and Jane can further her education at Oxford.

They both want to have children, but only after being married for at least two years. They have a plan. They have a calendar. They have a mutual understanding. They both have things they want, and they both have things they'll give up or contribute to make the marriage work.

A couple of years later, Jane and Dan have a small wedding in the backyard of Dan's family home. They don't spend much money on it. Jane has just started to work as a teacher. Dan is doing well, still working for someone else, but saving his money so he can start his own consulting firm. At the start of their marriage, they now have a solid financial nest egg to begin their lives together. They have two incomes, and when the time comes for Dan to quit his job and open his own firm, they'll be ready.

Dan and Jane, too, may not be twenty-five years old, but their future is markedly different than Jill and Ray's.

The difference is not that one husband was ambitious and one was not. The difference was that one couple was patient and thorough in dealing with relationship issues and one was not. The difference is the time they took to get to know each other, to go through a little bit of life together before getting married. There was also a difference in the preparation and planning that each couple invested prior to marriage, as well as the communication skills that each couple possessed, developed, and chose to use. The quality and consistency of the communication reduced the possibility for misunderstandings. It also provided a protocol for handling challenging times.

These factors contributed to the difference in outcomes between Jill and Ray, and Jane and Dan. Both couples were equally in love at the start, but only one couple remained happily married.

The Stages Of Life

The human species and its social structure have evolved over centuries. Today, in much of the developed world for many people, there are predictable stages of life that we can all recognize. Understanding these phases can provide a perspective about why, how, and when marriage fits into the grand scheme of things.

First, obviously, you're born. (Wink, nod.) In infancy, childhood, adolescence, and even young adulthood you may be completely dependent upon your parents or family structure for your physical needs, as well as your emotional needs. You are a student, most likely, attending school, but also learning about the world around you and how it functions. Your concerns seem large to you, but are really small. Your parents or older family members share the biggest responsibilities for making sure you're safe, fed, and cared for.

In young adulthood, you begin to make decisions for yourself. You choose a college and/or profession. You may decide where and how you want to live, how much money you want to make and what you want to do with it, what kind of 'lifestyle' you want to have. You have developed your personal identity to some extent. You may have sought adventure, taking an unusual vacation or working in an exotic location, doing something outside your comfort zone to test your limits. You may have developed career goals, dreams for life, and may have begun implementing them. You get your feet (fairly) firmly planted on the ground, and you're (somewhat) certain about the direction your life is going to take.

Then, you meet someone special. Or you suddenly realize that the 'best buddy' you've had for years is really the love of your life. You fall in love. Your relationship grows, develops, and matures. You and your partner decide you want to get married. Then, you decide where and how you want to live, how much money you want to make, and what you want to do with it—oh, right, all those things we talked about in the previous paragraph, only now, you're planning for two.

You marry, and then you may decide to have children. Most likely, you and your spouse become the breadwinners and providers for your child or children. Your extended family may or may not be in a position — emotionally, geographically, or financially — to help. You shoulder the responsibilities associated with being a husband, wife, mother, and father.

Your children grow, and soon they become young adults. They may leave home, start their own careers and families, and never return. Or they may encounter challenges and come to live with you again, or need money.

But, finally, there is the expectation that, at some point, you and your spouse can come full circle: a place where it's just the two of you, with, hopefully, enough financial security to pursue your dreams, whether they include travel, a second career, or charitable activities, and, perhaps, spending time with your grandchildren.

With a few revisions here and there, we can all recognize the lives of many people we know in this overview. It's a fairly natural progression that's based on a combination of societal and cultural factors, economic factors, and the evolution of human development and behavior over time.

Like the growth and development of the human body, and, really, all of nature, the growth and development of a person takes time. You can't rush it. Well, you can, but the results may not be what you'd hoped for. At the age of four, a child needs to play with toys and not be told the harsh realities of life. At the age of thirty-four, the toys should have been put away and a very comprehensive understanding of the world and its ways should be firmly in hand. Cultures and families have their own ways of leading a person from childhood to adulthood, with educational institutions, sports, religious rituals, family traditions, social functions, and the like.

We participate in these, sometimes reluctantly, and they change us, usually for the better. We're thrown into an environment where we don't know things. We are taught by teachers, mentors, peers, or experience. We learn. We are tested. We are transformed. We graduate, and then we move on. We apply what we've learned directly to our professions, or we simply appreciate the process for what it has added to our overall quality of life. This happens in school, the military, religious orders, on-the-job training, self-improvement endeavors, and social clubs.

These experiences are the difference between an eighteen year old college freshman and a twenty-two year old college graduate. One is still pretty much a kid, the other can lay claim to some credibility as an adult. Entering the workforce and learning from those experiences for ten years, the thirty-two year old who was once the college graduate should be even more mature.

Of course, people are individuals. Some are very mature at a very young age, and some never grow up. We've all seen that. But, on the whole, who is a better candidate to enter into marriage: the eighteen year old college freshman? Or the thirty-two year old with a college degree and ten years of work experience under his (or her) belt?

The answer is obvious. Why? Because there are certain things that only time and experience can do. When things in life are rushed or a process is truncated prematurely, it may have repercussions later. If a young man goes straight from high school, for example, directly into the military, does his tour of duty, and then is honorably discharged, he may not immediately be ready to be an employee, a husband, and a father. The fact that he may want to live as a bachelor, a student, a ranch hand, or a backpacker in Europe for a year or two is no character flaw. He simply hasn't had the opportunity to be on his own for a period of time with no pressing responsibilities. He may need to let the dust settle, in a manner of speaking, before he's ready to move onto the next stage of his life.

If you're in the student or young adult phase of life, cutting that short because you want or have to get married can seriously impact your life and all of your relationships. This, too, is obvious, but it's worth stating. The list of things and people you may resent as a result can be a long one: you may resent your spouse for pressuring you into it; you may resent your parents and friends for not talking you out of it; you may resent your child for limiting your opportunities. That's no way to live.

To the extent that you fully experience each stage of life is probably going to be the extent that you fully enjoy all of life. When you're a child, be a child. Hopefully, events will not conspire to make your childhood traumatic or force you into the responsibility of adulthood prematurely. When you're a student, be a student. Study, laugh, learn, explore, question, challenge, dream. But don't rush into adulthood, if at all possible, by starting a family or getting married before you're prepared to.

Understand, honor, and respect nature and its processes. The stages of life that are a part of our existence are natural, sometimes slow, but critical to our success in life, love, and marriage. I've discussed the stages of life at the start of this book on marriage for several reasons.

Here they are:

- ♥ You have to know where you are before you can chart a course to go somewhere else;

- ♥ You have to articulate and acknowledge the path that you've taken, the journey you've experienced, and understand how it's affected and shaped you before you can credibly commit to another person for a lifetime; and

- ♥ You have to let go of your garbage in order to make room for your treasure.

The result that can come from this awareness is that you can sit down with your potential spouse and say, "This is how I grew up, what I experienced, how I think it impacted me, how I felt really blessed and then how I felt a little (or a lot) short-changed, and how I want to make sure that our life together absolutely has this in it and absolutely does not have this in it."

You'll be out of breath after that run-on sentence, but, in saying it, you'll have done more to start your relationship off on solid ground than most couples. Some couples have haphazard conversations like this late at night, in the car, after making love, here and there, with varying amounts of real communication and understanding.

With an issue as important as marriage, I suggest that you write this stuff down. Ask your potential spouse to write it down. Then sit down in a dedicated space and without interruption, discuss what you've written down. Second, and even more importantly, listen to what your potential spouse has to say. If they tell you that their childhood was marred with anxiety about financial insecurity due to their parents' behavior, that's an important emotional issue that you will have to prioritize in order to make your marriage work.

So you'll be reading your list of how you grew up, what you experienced, and how you think it shaped you, but, more importantly, you'll be listening and writing down the things that are important to your potential spouse. If you can't listen to your potential spouse, understand what they're saying *and how they feel about what they're saying,* and make choices, and perhaps changes in your behavior, to show you're aware and that you care, you're not ready for marriage.

Again, if you can't listen to your potential spouse's important issues and honestly see yourself making choices or reaching a mutually satisfying arrangement or compromise to accommodate their feelings, then you're not ready to marry this particular person, *no matter how much you love them right now.*

During the life of your marriage, you're going to consistently make choices and take actions that put the feelings of your spouse first. Your spouse, in turn, is going to do the same for you. You're not going to have sex with other people. You're not going to spend money any way you please. You are going to make allowances for family members, yours and your spouse's. You're not going to abuse alcohol, drugs, your spouse, or your children. You're going to 'have their back' and they're going to have yours. *This is, to put it indelicately, the deal.*

This is a long road and a lot of work, but it is beyond worth it in so many ways and on so many levels. The first thing you must do, however, is take an inventory of yourself. What you've been through and where you're at. Be honest with yourself first. Be honest with your spouse, too.

You do that by assessing what stage of life you're currently in, if you've ticked all the boxes in your previous stages, so to speak, so that you don't feel like you've missed out on anything. If you feel like you've done it all as a child, adolescent, or young adult, or if you truly feel alright about the things you didn't get to do, at that point, you might be ready for marriage.

Questions to Ask and Answer

- ♥ What stage of life am I experiencing right now?

- ♥ Looking back, do I feel like any stage of my life was cut short? Was any stage extended too long, beyond what is healthy?

- ♥ Were these time periods a direct result of a choice I made? Or were these choices made by my family? Were these circumstances beyond anyone's control?

- ♥ Looking at my present situation, do I feel any resentment or see any repercussions that have resulted from a stage of my life not being fully experienced?

- ♥ Do I blame myself for the choices I made? Do I blame my family? Do I blame God?

- ♥ Is blaming anyone for anything helping me live a fuller life? Or is it holding me back?

- ♥ Can I fix or revisit an issue in a stage of life that I feel I didn't experience fully? (For example, if your education was cut short due to a family obligation, can you now go back to school?)

- ♥ Can I let go of any and all resentment about a stage of my life not being fully experienced?

- ♥ Can I accept responsibility for what might happen in my life if I don't let go of these resentments?

- ♥ Can I change the past?

- ♥ Can I change the future, other than by making choices and taking action in the present moment?

Your Childhood Experience

You probably experienced your first impressions of marriage during childhood. If you didn't have two parents in your home, you probably had friends who had two parents who were married, or married members within your extended family. You saw how marriage worked, or didn't work, for your parents or other adult couples. You may have recognized differences in how couples relate to one another.

This experience gave you a model with certain characteristics which you consciously or subconsciously chose to embrace, reject, or consider. Many psychologists have researched the ideas that men grow up to marry their mothers and women grow up wanting to marry Daddy. I have no idea how much of that is accurate, but there's no doubting the influence that our childhood has on our views of marriage.

I will say this: it may be very difficult for a person who has not experienced love, trust, comfort, security, and responsible behavior as a young child to commit to another person for a lifetime. Nevertheless, I see it happen every day. It happens because being loved by someone and loving another person can change an individual in unimaginable ways. Love is a transformative phenomenon.

Still, you will want to fully examine what you think, feel, and hope for in marriage. While some of these ideas you have are the result of your educational, cultural, and social experiences, many of them are rooted in childhood. Witnessing very unpleasant behavior between parents as a child can make the grown child dogmatic about certain issues. If the family was very tight with money and reserved in expressing love, those two issues may have become confused in the perception of the now-adult child. This person may spend freely or even irresponsibly, and be sexually promiscuous, wanting to express their emotions or have love (or something like it) expressed to them in return.

Without becoming excessively self-involved, we should identify and address our childhood issues and experiences that relate to marriage. We need to identify our first role models. They may have been our parents. What did we see that we liked about their relationship? What was unhealthy about it? What techniques or strategies did they use with each other to get through difficult times, like the death of a loved one or a financial setback? What behavior did they use that was manipulative? How often did they celebrate? How did they celebrate? How did they compromise? How did they make up after a disagreement?

This may be difficult, as we can still be childlike as we look at our parents, but if you're going to fashion a solid and fulfilling marriage for yourself and your spouse, you need to take what you've seen and experienced and consciously decide if you want to repeat it. If you don't do this consciously, you risk acting out in your marriage, for better or worse, unconsciously.

You probably want to repeat or model some of the behavior you saw in your parents' marriage, but not all of it. Then, once you've noted and refined your desired behaviors, you can take ideas of your own and add on to it. What you add to it are things important to you emotionally and have nothing to do with your parents.

You'll also want to articulate how these behaviors and habits that your parents engaged in, good and bad, *made you feel*. Once you identify the incident and the emotion, you can process your feelings. These feelings may be at the root of some less than desirable behavior you're exhibiting in your own relationship. Identifying them may help you and your relationship. They may be good memories, as well, and may be the reason you can love confidently and communicate effectively. You don't want to lose those qualities, and your spouse certainly doesn't want you to lose them. So know them all, good and bad. Discard the bad after you've processed your feelings. Embrace the good and move forward.

As you consider marrying someone, you obviously understand that you are marrying that person. What you also need to understand is that you are marrying that child. The emotional landscape that forms their personality was shaped by their earliest impressions as a child, just as yours was. The most vivid and long-lasting of those impressions are probably about things that happened in their home, involving the people they were closest to.

One of the key steps in getting to know someone is to meet their family. This is a time-honored ritual, and almost a routine matter as couples move forward in their relationship. (I'll discuss this later.) Perhaps just as important is to go back to their childhood home. Visit the neighborhood your potential spouse grew up in. Listen to their stories. Get a glimpse of the child that is now the adult. This will help you understand more about your potential mate than will hours of conversation. You want to intimately understand your partner's childhood through listening to what they say, but also, just as critically, experiencing their world. We don't enter a relationship in a bubble. We're a product of our childhoods, our neighborhoods, our schools, our friends, and our culture.

Share your childhood memories and photos together. Take your time. Get to know the adult and the child. Confide your most vivid childhood memories to your partner. Come clean. Give them as clear a picture of you as a child as you possibly can, and, without prying or violating their privacy, try to get as clear a picture of their childhood as you can.

I emphasize this because when you marry, you will be born again, as a child, into a new world, with another child, your partner. Your parents gave you protection, love, and comfort as a child. Now, you will do that for your partner. And they will do that for you.

Marriage is a risk, usually a public one. Everyone knows you're getting married or that you are married. You're very excited and a little scared. You are emotionally vulnerable, just like a child. So remember to be tender with your partner, as you would a child. Not condescending, not manipulative, but gentle. Trust them with all your heart, as a child does. And be trustworthy. Hold hands, like children do, and venture forth.

You will know the best and worst of your partner. They will know your weaknesses, fears, and disappointments. You will both know how to make each other soar, and how to destroy each other if you wish. You will take comfort in their love and take strength from their loyalty. You will, childlike, share untold secrets and experience unimaginable joys. You will live, much of the time, in your own little world that unmarried people may publicly scoff at, but privately envy. It will begin in a very childlike way, and if you are lucky, it will continue that same way throughout your lives together.

So it's important to know the child you are, and the child you are marrying.

Questions to Ask and Answer

- What are my first memories or images of married people?
- Were they my parents?
- How do I feel when I remember, as a child, seeing my parents together?
- What feelings did I have when my parents divorced?
- How much of an influence has television and film had on my idea of marriage?
- How have the marriages of members of my family, like siblings, uncles, or aunts, had an impact on the way I see marriage?
- What will I absolutely not tolerate in a marriage?
- What must I absolutely have in a marriage?
- Was there abuse in my parents' marriage? Was it substance abuse? Verbal abuse? Physical abuse?
- How did I feel when I experienced it or heard about it as a child?
- What was the best part of my parents' marriage?
- Was there trust in my parents' marriage?
- Did I feel like they prioritized my well-being? Or were they more interested in their own well-being?
- What need do I think my mother fulfilled for my father? What need did he fulfill for her?
- What childhood need do I think a spouse will fulfill for me?

Your Education Experience

The length, quality, and scope of your education experience are critical factors in determining the quality and duration of your marriage.

A study done by the US Department of Labor Statistics in 2014 showed the divorce rate for college graduates was 26.5%, while the divorce rate for those with some college was 42.3%. Those with only a high school diploma divorced at a 42.8% rate, and those with only some high school were at 47.8%.

Those are statistics, based on numbers. There are conclusions that could logically be drawn from these statistics, and they may help you as you decide when and whom to marry.

The first conclusion might be that college graduates marry later than other groups studied because they are still in college until their early twenties. So, to a certain extent, it might be better to marry a little later in life if you want to have a good shot at staying married.

You're older, maybe more mature, maybe a little wiser. You've probably had a chance to date and get to know a larger number of potential partners. You've probably established yourself a little more firmly in your career. You have a better sense of who you are. And, sad to say, but true just the same, you've had the chance to watch other people make mistakes and you've learned from those.

The second conclusion might be that higher education provides not only technical knowledge that can benefit your professional life, but also psychological development, social skills, and interpersonal skills that can help in married life. Certainly, being thrown into a new, unfamiliar environment like a college campus pulls on mental and emotional resources and expands horizons. It always has and always will. Meeting people who are completely different than you and discovering that you have a lot in common is life-changing. Being required to live with someone you don't know in a small dorm room for nine months at a time might build relationship and cohabitation skills.

The third conclusion is that higher education changes a person's perception of themselves and their relationship to others. Perhaps it makes them more empathetic, more flexible, more tolerant. It certainly is likely to provide them with more tools, in terms of vocabulary and concepts, with which they can articulate their feelings and understand the feelings of others. They may learn, through the study of literature and history, that they are not the first generation to feel frustrated and angry at the status quo. They are not the first group to experience a feeling of anxiety about the future. They are not the first person to know and try to express the feelings of romantic love. While this understanding that others around the world and throughout the ages have felt what we feel may not offer answers, it can offer a sense of perspective and comfort as we try to find a solution.

The fourth conclusion might be that college graduates generally have more job opportunities and more upward mobility than non-college graduates. While this assumption may be challenged in today's economic environment, it has certainly been true in the past, and may be true again in the future.

This could mean that college graduates have the potential for fewer financial problems in life and, consequently, in marriage. Certainly, most college students live on a budget, many for the first time, when they leave the comforts of home and go away to school. This skill, living on a certain amount of money for a certain period of time, is honed and (hopefully) perfected by the time a person graduates from college. This is especially true with those who work to put themselves through college and deal with the repayment of student loans.

The fifth conclusion that could be reached is that college graduates understand the concept of a process. A process being something that is approached with preparation, addressed incrementally, and accomplished in stages over time. It involves getting feedback on progress, perhaps experiencing failure, succeeding at short-term tasks, and keeping your eyes on a long-term goal. The process of going to college and obtaining a degree involves becoming part of a process, of giving yourself over to the unknown in hopes of experiencing something worthwhile, becoming a bigger and better person, and securing something of value through your own efforts.

The education process requires that, first of all, you acknowledge that you don't know everything. (Wink, nod.) There must also be a willingness to learn. At some point, the opportunity will present itself to apply what you have learned in a real-world environment, or at least during a test. You will have to learn to work with others, learn from those who know more than you, and even learn from those who know less than you. You will have to think critically and creatively. You will want to master what you're naturally very good at, but you will still need to become competent at things you hate doing and don't do well at all. You will have too little time to do many things, but you still must endeavor to do them well.

Remember, too, that the education process does not stop when you graduate from college, just as the process of marriage does not stop when the wedding has concluded. That's when it begins. Many people like the idea of *getting married*. It's a bridal shower, and a bachelor party, and a wedding, and a honeymoon, and playing house as newlyweds. Fewer have what it takes to be married, day in and day out, and *enjoy the process*.

My advice is to get an education. If a formal education is out of reach or in the rearview mirror, conceive, begin, and maintain a course of independent study and personal improvement for yourself. Read at least a book a month, and not trash. Read for pleasure. Read to be more informed. Read to be transformed.

Second, spend your discretionary dollars on travel, which is an education unto itself. I'm not talking about Las Vegas or a cheap cruise. I'm talking about visiting and really experiencing places with history and culture different from your own.

Third, if at all possible, make sure your potential spouse has the same, or close to the same, level and quality of education as you do. If they do not, ascertain if they have the same attitude about education and its importance as you do. This will not only impact your life, but the lives of any children you might have during the course of your marriage.

How you and your potential spouse perceive education is a critical issue in the success of your marriage. If you see the value in it and they don't, you're in trouble, and so are your children.

Questions to Ask and Answer

♥ Am I dating a person who shares basically the same level of education as I do?

♥ Am I dating a person who places basically the same value on education as I do?

♥ Will the person I'm dating want to set aside money for our children's education? Or will they want to spend it on consumer items?

♥ What is my family history with regards to education? Am I the first person to graduate from college? Does my family have a generation or two of college graduates?

♥ What is my potential spouse's family history with regards to education? Are his parents college graduates? Are his siblings?

♥ Did I attend college with my potential spouse?

♥ Did I see his study habits?

♥ Does my potential partner read for pleasure?

♥ Does he or she discuss things they've read or are reading?

♥ What book or books have changed my life?

♥ What book or books have changed my partner's life?

♥ Do I see myself watching television every night with my spouse? Or do I see us watching some television some nights and reading some nights?

Your Friends
And Family

It is most likely that you will have known your friends and family longer and more intimately than you have known the person you are considering marrying. Your friends and family know you very well, and have probably seen you grow and change as a person over time. In healthy relationships, they have a concern for your well-being and a sense of what is good for you and what is not.

If you're like most people, your friends and family compose a large part of your emotional world. You've grown up with them. You've fought with them. You've celebrated with them. You've laughed with them. You've cried with them. They generally genuinely want what is best for you. They want you to be happy. There is usually a considerable bond of loyalty. There is usually love.

At some point in time during the dating process, it is wise to introduce your partner to your friends and family. Your partner will also, at some point, probably introduce you to their friends and family. This ritual is entertaining fodder for numerous television shows and movies, but do not underestimate the importance of it. I stated earlier that you 'marry the child.' I will also say now that you 'marry the family.'

When you introduce your potential mate to your parents, everyone is probably going to try to be on their best behavior. There's a natural anticipation in the air that may border on anxiety. At some level, you, as your parents' child, want their approval regarding the person that you're considering spending the rest of your life with. Your parents, because they probably love you, are hopeful that you've made a choice that will make you happy. But, they are also human. They want to be happy with your choice, too. So they're going to be very curious, very circumspect, and very protective.

The same can probably be said for your siblings, extended family, and friends. They will be making casual conversation on the surface with your potential partner at a social gathering, but make no mistake: they will be laser-focused on getting a genuine sense of your partner and deciding if they are a good person and a good match for you. Sometimes their questions will be couched in delicate and diplomatic language. Sometimes the interrogation will make the Spanish Inquisition look like a church social.

At some point after introductions and conversation, one of your friends or family members is going to quietly circle back to you and offer their opinion about your potential partner. This is one of the trickiest moments in life, for several reasons. First, they want to be supportive and be happy for you. They want to like this person that you like and maybe love. They want to say nice things about him or her. So, they might do that just to spare your feelings and hope that you'll see that this person is not the genuine article before you make too much of a commitment. Or they may sincerely like the person and think you've made a good choice.

That's one friend or family member. The other is going to tell you flat out that this guy or girl is no good for you, or, in more measured terms, not the best choice you could make. The danger here is that you'll be offended, even if they're right, and you'll lose a friend or be upset with a family member. Your job is to take whatever your friends or family say in stride. Digest it. Don't react. Take your time. Sleep on it. Think about it.

You'll try to determine if there's a hidden agenda or personal issue woven in with their comments. You'll try to read between the lines. It's nerve-racking, but it's necessary. There's an old saying that proclaims, 'You can fool all of the people some of the time, and some of the people all of the time, but you can't fool all of the people all of the time.' And that's why you go through the ulcer-inducing process of introducing your potential mate to your friends and family. This is the person you care about, and it's been said that love is blind. If there are things about your potential partner that you can't or won't see, your friends and family will most likely see it. They're looking at him or her with a distanced, cautious, and critical eye.

So you need to listen to what they say. Ask them why they think what they do. If two or more of them are not thrilled about your choice, you need to know why. Then you've got some hard thinking to do, because the people that know you best and who may or probably have your best interests at heart see trouble up ahead.

A strong word of advice: do not have these conversations over alcohol in a pub. Have them over coffee and in private.

Here is the first scenario: you really like your partner, and your friends really like your partner. Find out why. Get real answers and observations from them about how your partner interacted with them in a social setting. Was it how he or she handled an awkward moment gracefully? How much did they have to drink? Were they especially attentive to or patient with an elderly guest? Why? Because your potential partner may act one way around you and another way around your friends, especially if alcohol is involved. You need to find out now if their behavior is consistent and above board.

Second scenario: you like your partner and one or two of your friends or family members out of, let's say, ten, have their reservations. You could put this down to personality differences, which could be ironed out in time. Not everyone in a family or group of friends absolutely adores everyone else. This arithmetic is not a deal-breaker, but it is something to think about.

Third scenario: you like your partner and your friends and family members are hesitant or outright concerned. If the phrase, 'Oh, hell, no,' comes up from numerous friends or family members, you have some soul-searching to do. Either you have made a serious error in judgment, or you will have to consider marrying and living with someone that your friends and family members do not care for. And again, you have to solicit and listen to the reasoning behind their concerns. One of the most difficult to digest will be,

'He just doesn't feel right.' This will be difficult to process because intuition usually arrives with the least evidence and often the most accuracy.

We've been speaking in terms of the initial meeting between your friends and family members and your potential spouse. This interaction should be repeated as often as possible in order for you, your partner, and your friends and family to get a more comprehensive and fair assessment of each other.

This process needs to happen before you make any kind of serious commitment to your partner. You will probably be dating them exclusively at this point. That's all. Unless you're trying to distance yourself from your friends and family, you don't get engaged and you certainly don't get married before introducing your partner to your friends and family.

Know this: any potential partner who pressures you to run away and get married, and then surprise your friends and family with the news is up to no good. This is a red flag. Run for the hills. Any partner who subtly or overtly tries to separate you from your friends and family and isolate you is up to no good. This is a red flag. Run for the hills. Any partner who claims to not have any family or friends to introduce you to is up to no good. Run for the hills. Any potential partner who wants to discuss money — yours or theirs — prematurely, or wants to discuss business ventures with your family members or friends, is up to no good. Run for the hills. Any potential partner who says he doesn't like your drunk Uncle Elliot is just being honest. No flag at all. Not to worry.

Now we'll discuss the scenario where you meet your partner's friends and family. Understandably, you're a little nervous. This is a symptom of something being important to you and important to the person you care about. Your partner's family will probably be curious about you and what your interests and plans are. Less directly, they will be trying to see what stage your relationship with their child is currently at and how healthy it is.

Everything that your friends and family did when your partner visited with them is now happening to you: the questions, the assessments, the approving nod or the suspiciously arched eyebrow. But you're not worried: your potential spouse is attentive, supportive, and affectionate. You'll be fine.

What you should be keenly aware of is that this is not simply an event to be dreaded and, perhaps, endured. It is an opportunity for you to discover your potential partner's most intimate emotional world: his family and his friends. These family members are the people who raised him, shaped him, and educated him. They were his role models. He learned the rules of life and the rules of love from them. He is likely to share their attributes as well as their faults. He shares their DNA.

No less important are the friends he chose. These are the people whose opinions and feelings matter to him. He shares their values and their morals. He confides in them, and. to some extent, he admires them and is like them.

If you marry, it is likely that you will spend a considerable amount of time with these people. If they are malicious, cruel, insensitive, and rude, and you think your potential spouse is the only one who's different, the one good apple in the whole bunch, think again. If his parents are inconsiderate of each other, consider that. Watch how he and his siblings interact. That's how he'll interact with you in a few years, regardless of what feelings you have now for each other and how he treats you right now in the early spring of a relationship.

I don't encourage you to enter into relations with your potential in-laws like a character in an Edwardian novel, sizing up the rich and crazy aunt, verbally jousting with the siblings, and taking a cold and calculated assessment of everyone and everything you see. I do intend for you to pay attention to more than just your immediate feelings for the person you care about.

Love is a critical part of marriage. There's no substitute for that spark, that chemistry, that magic that poets bleed about, that singers and musicians call to the stars about, that teenagers giggle about, and that octogenarians wax nostalgic about. But that feeling is only a single aspect of this overreaching endeavor. One reason that the divorce rate is so high in America, in my opinion, is that young couples don't take enough time and apply enough rational thought as to how well they're going to fit into each other's existing lives as they create their own new lives together.

Yes, you're in love. I'm happy for you. I'm in love, too, and I have been for over a quarter of a century, to the same woman. We achieved this enduring harmony by entering our marriage with our heads as well as our hearts.

I'm not saying that your new love's family has to be perfect. A lot of great people emerge from less-than-wonderful home environments. They often become passionate about creating a home that was entirely different from the one they grew up in. They want a loving, secure, and safe family life. And a lot of really confused and unhappy people spring from photo-op family settings. They never recognize, grasp, or appreciate the blessings they had growing up.

The important thing is that you know the landscape from which your potential partner has come and realize that it is one of the landscapes that the two of you will share to some extent if you marry.

Questions to ask and answer

- What are the things you like about your partner's family?
- What are the things you don't like?
- Who are the family members that you think you'll be closest to?
- Do you feel like your partner fits in with your friends and family?
- Do you feel like you fit in with his?
- How were you received initially by his friends? Were they polite? Cool?
- How did your friends respond to meeting your partner?
- After meeting his friends and family, do you look forward to seeing them again?
- Would you be happy if you ended up in a marriage that resembled the marriage his parents have?
- If your partner has siblings, what are their relationships and marriages like? Successful? Strained?
- Is there a history of physical abuse or substance abuse in his family?
- Did his friends and family talk about money in a social setting? How little they had? How much they had?
- If children were present at the gathering, were they polite and well-mannered? Whose children were they?

Your Social Class

Here it is: the 'C' word. To many people, referring to a person's social class smacks of elitism. It's condescending. We live, after all, in America, the world's first truly classless society. Upward mobility is our defining concept. Anybody can work hard and prosper. Anyone can grow up to be a millionaire or even a billionaire. Anyone can be President of the United States.

All the statements above may have a large measure of truth to them. However, the fact remains that most societies in the world have social classes, and America is no different. We're not all middle class, as we like to think. Our society, like others around the world, has blue-collar workers, white-collar executives, entrepreneurs, artists, writers, and those who have been wealthy for an extended period of time. That's a broad picture of the social terrain that anthropologists and sociologists spend years researching, analyzing, and writing about. Feel free to disagree with me, but also feel free to nod along in recognition if you read anything that's familiar.

People in different social classes have different tastes, values, priorities, and ambitions. I'll speak briefly in general terms about each.

Blue-collar workers prioritize job security. They want to make a reasonable wage and enjoy employment benefits, and they want to be appreciated for the work they do. They're comfortable with the predictable, routine nature of their jobs and embrace challenges and change gradually. The scope of their work is defined. They want employment and social benefits to protect them against accident, injury, or illness, and rightly so. Their vacations are set by company policy. They hope to be able to retire financially secure.

Blue-collar workers usually graduate from high school, but may not have attended or graduated from college. Some have college degrees. They will marry in their early twenties. Home ownership is a big goal for them. With discretionary income (above expenses and perhaps some savings), they purchase consumer products. They watch several hours of television per day. They will socialize with friends, family, and coworkers for pleasure. They will travel locally or regionally. Their children attend public schools. They may dress up to go to church, but, generally, they wear casual clothes or work clothes, which may be the same thing. Around the house, they may or may not be fully clothed. When going out in public, they may or may not be well-dressed or well-groomed. If they receive a financial windfall, they may buy new consumer products with it and celebrate with friends.

White-collar workers, entrepreneurs, artists, and writers have probably attended and graduated from college. They prioritize job satisfaction and opportunity for advancement in their careers. They want to make as high a salary as possible. They want to advance in their career, have control over their future, and contribute to their given industry, business, genre, or art. The scope of their work is somewhat defined, but elements of it can be constantly in flux. They also want some benefits from their work and society, but their focus is on doing more and earning more. Many are self-employed. They do not think about retirement in defined terms. They are doing what they love and will never retire from work. Others will choose a second career at some point and work just as hard at that as they did the first career.

This social class will invest discretionary income and prioritize their financial independence. They will marry in their late twenties to early thirties. Their children's education will be more important than purchasing consumer products. They will read books consistently and socialize for work and pleasure. They will travel internationally.

They will wear business attire if they are executives, and anything they want if they are entrepreneurs, writers, or artists. Casual attire for executives leans toward a 'preppy' look. This social class generally gets dressed even if they are not going out. In public, they are usually presentable, but with writers and artists, you never know. If they receive a financial windfall, they may invest part of it and purchase recognizable and status-heavy products or a new residence to communicate their new position in society.

Those who have had wealth, education, and privilege for three generations or more comprise what has been referred to as the 'upper class.' I refer to them as Old Money. They prioritize wealth preservation and quality of life. In this regard, they can be conservative in their views as they might think that the status quo is a good thing to maintain. They also know the importance of stability in society. In this regard, they can be liberal in their views as they might think that creating opportunities and providing for the well-being of others not as financially well-off is a good thing to promote.

This social class either inherits a business or investments which they oversee or expand, or they pursue a career of their own choosing. The career they choose may or may not be lucrative. It is, generally speaking, simply what they love to do. Family insurance policies or assets protect them from the financial consequences of accident, injury, illness, or unemployment. With discretionary income, they reinvest or travel. They are infrequent purchasers of consumer products, as their houses, cars, and clothing tend to be traditional, well-maintained, and well-worn. Their children are educated at private schools and may study abroad. With a financial windfall, nothing in their lives really changes.

As I've said, I've painted with some really broad strokes here. Exceptions to these profiles will be easy to find. Disagreeing with or being able to justifiably revise the characteristics of these groups would be an equally easy thing to do. Proving me wrong is an easy thing to do. I'm wrong a lot, just, you know, not about this. (Wink, nod.)

If you're honest, you can probably see yourself in one of these three categories. I'm not saying that you are not an individual. I'm not saying that your life has less or more value than anyone else's. I'm not saying what is or is not possible for you in this life. Everybody gets born into a family. That's not your choice. That family has circumstances, some good, some bad. Again, not your choice.

The big choice has been how you've responded to the circumstances of your birth. That's what your life has been about, in the grand scheme of things. Now, we're looking at this particular issue. Now, the choice you have is whether or not you're going to acknowledge your background so you can make a smart choice about your future. You want to make a smart choice about marriage, which is probably the biggest choice of your life.

How honest and thorough are you going to be with yourself about this subject?

I hit this subject hard because people tend to think it doesn't matter or that discussing social class is being elitist. It's not. Your background is a part of who you are. It defines the way you see the world. It shapes what you think is important. *Your background doesn't limit you unless you allow it to, but it does color your world.*

If you are ambitious and you want to leave a blue-collar life and experience a white-collar life, that's great. I would simply encourage you to make sure that your potential spouse wants the same thing. Also, know the dangers of a partnership predicated on upward social and financial mobility: if, ten years into the marriage, you're not climbing the proverbial ladder at the rate you'd imagined, is it over?

If you want to marry below your social class, know that your spouse may have major adjustments to make in terms of fitting in with your family, friends, and work colleagues. You will also have to adjust as you spend time with in-laws and new friends.

If you are marrying above your social class, you will need to learn the customs and manners of the class you are marrying into. It may be stressful for you and your marriage, but if you know that and still want to marry, do so.

You should also know this: social class has nothing to do with race or national identity. Old Money in America and Old Money in Mexico, Hong Kong, or Africa all act, speak, dress, and conduct their lives in pretty much the same manner.

Social class is not all about money, either. Everyone has experienced or seen media coverage about New Money and how different it is from Old Money. A blue-collar person can make a lot of money, but without other factors playing into their life, they will not become members of a different social class. An upper-class person may be living on a very middle-class professor's salary, but if other values and factors are maintained, they will not leave their social class.

Certain social classes have certain values, priorities, and habits. The social class that we are born into shapes us more than we will ever know. In light of these realities, I would recommend that you do two things:

First, marry someone within your social class. You will have more in common than you realize. You're probably going to share the same perspectives on many subjects because you've shared many of the same experiences. You've probably been raised in similar environments as children, adolescents, and young adults. Obviously, if someone is exactly like you, they will irritate you to no end. But if someone is very, very different than you, you may have difficulty understanding 'where they're coming from' on important issues in life. This is tricky business in a marriage.

These 'class' factors contribute to form shared values, priorities, and habits that will be the foundation upon which you navigate opportunities, risks, challenges, disagreements, and misunderstandings. Problems with extended family will be reduced. Issues with money, children, and leisure will be easier to deal with. You both will 'be on the same page' with so many of the things that you, as a married couple, face throughout your lives together.

Second, discuss in detail whether the two of you want to go through life and remain in your social class, or strive for upward mobility. Both of you must agree to what you want to do in this regard. If you do not agree, your marriage will have a smaller chance of success. One spouse will not understand the longer working hours of an ambitious partner. Another partner may not understand the easy-going attitude of their spouse with regards to career advancement, accumulation or preservation of wealth, or even steady employment.

There is absolutely nothing wrong with starting out in life as a blue-collar couple and ending up that way fifty years later. The success of your marriage is not measured by how much you moved up the social ladder. But the success of your marriage may be dependent to a large extent on the shared social class of you and your partner.

Questions to Ask and Answer

- Based on the information provided in this chapter, what social class do you honestly believe you belong to?

- What factors or experiences make you believe you belong to a certain social class?

- Are you comfortable with you social class?

- Do you want to change your social class?

- Do you want your children to have the opportunity to belong to another social class?

- From what you know about your potential spouse, do they belong to the same social class as you?

- What makes you think so?

- Did you meet your potential spouse in college?

- Were either of you a member of a fraternity or sorority?

- Do you and your potential spouse share the same set of friends? Did your parents or families know each other prior to your relationship starting?

- Did you and your potential spouse grow up in the same city? The same neighborhood?

- If you grew up in different cities, but had grown up in the same city, would it be likely that you would have grown up in the same neighborhood?

- What are the educational, economic, and professional backgrounds of your parents? What those of your potential spouse's parents?

- If you receive a financial windfall during the course of your marriage, what will you want to do with it? What will your spouse want to do with it?

- ♥ How much television do you watch on a daily basis?

- ♥ How many books do you read on a monthly basis?

- ♥ Is shopping a social event for you? Or is it something you do only when you really need to buy something?

- ♥ How often do you shop? How often do you go online to buy things that are not necessities? How often do you go to shopping mall or retail area?

- ♥ Do you watch shopping channels on television? Do you purchase things you see advertised there?

- ♥ Do you purchase and wear the latest fashions? Or do you purchase clothing that you wear year after year?

- ♥ If you want to change social classes, why do you want to do that?

- ♥ What sacrifices are you willing to make to do that?

- ♥ How does your potential spouse feel about and answer the two previous questions?

- ♥ If you had to choose between buying a new home or saving money for your children's education, which would you choose?

- ♥ When you think of 'rich people' or 'upper-class' people, how do you feel?

- ♥ Do you 'get dressed up' only when the occasion warrants it? Or do you get dressed in what might be termed 'business casual' most days, regardless of what events or plans you have?

- ♥ How structured was your family life when you were growing up? Were meals eaten at the dining table or kitchen table? Or were they eaten in front of the television?

- ♥ Were there books in your home as you grew up?

Your Values

Your childhood, your education, your social class — all these have combined to shape your values. Your values, like the noun 'value', the adjective 'valuable', and the verb 'to value', refer to something that you consider worthwhile and important, something of substance. These are things you feel are worth preserving, enhancing, communicating to others, and taking a stand for. (I do realize that I end sentences with a preposition. I don't really care.)

In "The Old Money Book", I discussed the Core Values of Old Money. If you haven't read that book or don't instantly recall these values, here they are:

- ♥ Health
- ♥ Education
- ♥ The Work Ethic
- ♥ Etiquette and Manners
- ♥ Financial Independence
- ♥ Family and Marriage, and
- ♥ Privacy

Most people would agree in conversation that these are good things to value in life. However, the thing that I must mention is that I advocate *adopting the values, priorities, and habits* of Old Money in order to live a richer life. Paying lip service to the values I've listed above is little help to improving your quality of life. When you truly adopt these values, you rearrange your priorities. These priorities change your behavior, and over time create new habits. This process alters your life, slowly, permanently, and for the better.

So, how do values relate to marriage? They are the basis for the choices you and your spouse are going to make, individually and jointly. They are the blueprint that you consciously or unconsciously refer to prior to thinking something, saying something, or doing something. They affect how you spend your time, your money, and your life. And, as I've said, they affect the quality of your life.

Therefore, I would sincerely encourage you to assess your values first. Second, I would suggest that you assess the values of your potential spouse. When you have done this, you can compare your findings and determine to a large extent how harmonious your marriage will be. Much of the accuracy of this assessment will be contingent upon how honest you are with yourself.

You should also be aware that, over time, you will be influenced by your spouse's values and they will be influenced by yours. Furthermore, people can think that they hold certain values and tell you that they hold certain values and believe in certain things, then behave in a way that is inconsistent with those values and beliefs. This can be the result of delusion, outright dishonesty, or rationalization.

The human brain rationalizes behavior that it finds inconsistent with its closely-held values. We all know what is right and what is wrong. We have a sense of that, even as children. When we do something wrong, we either have to accept that behavior, which makes us feel badly about ourselves, or we can rationalize it. Sometimes our rationale has merit. If someone is breaking into our house and has a gun, and we have a gun and shoot them, we claim self-defense. We have taken a life, but under the circumstances, our behavior can be acceptable to us and others.

Sometimes we don't connect behavior with values. A person can say, 'Yes, I value health.' But if he smokes cigarettes and drinks heavily, we know he's not being honest with himself. He's not equating what he (perhaps) believes and what he (actually) says with what he (habitually) does. Somewhere, there is a deception or a disconnect in the process. This person may be delusional.

The problem may be the self-image the person has forged, which is how they see and value themselves. Do they value themselves enough to be honest with themselves? Note: everybody has work to do in this area. We can all improve the way we see ourselves and what we say to ourselves. I'm not suggesting that you not marry someone because they aren't perfect. I'm suggesting you take a hard look at what's important to you and make sure your potential spouse is pretty much on board with the same ideals.

If health is important to you, my guess is that your exercise regularly. You probably eat fresh foods in moderation. You don't abuse alcohol, tobacco, or recreational pharmaceuticals. You see a dentist and doctor regularly to make sure nothing creeps up on you, and, if it does, you nip it in the bud, so to speak. You generally lead an active life. Your hobbies involve doing something physical, probably outside, at least a few times a week.

If this doesn't describe your life, then you may be under a doctor's care right now, working to get an injury, disease, or condition alleviated so you can get back to this kind of life. Or you may be physically handicapped and unable to lead this kind of life, and you're being as healthy as you can be. Otherwise, health is not a priority for you, no matter what you think or say to yourself or others.

It's that simple. If you just don't prioritize health, I have no idea why that is. I would only suggest that you marry someone else who doesn't prioritize health. The reason I say this is that a healthy person with healthy habits is going to grow very weary very quickly of an unhealthy person who doesn't work to maintain their health. Why? Because the healthy spouse will be the one taking care of the unhealthy spouse. Of course, everyone gets sick. Illness is a part of life. When your spouse gets sick or injured through no fault of their own, it's distressing beyond words. That's not what I'm talking about here. I'm talking about habits that contribute to or take away from health in particular and quality of life in general.

Understanding that your behavior, rooted in values, impacts not just you but your spouse and possibly your children, makes it critical to address your feelings about the values I've mentioned, not just health. You can then ascertain the degree to which you and your spouse are compatible in this regard.

You and your potential spouse should share values that contribute to your individual and joint quality of life. These values are not concepts you say you embrace. They are what your daily actions and habits proclaim you embrace. If you say you value something and consistently behave in a contrary manner, you are either lying to yourself, lying to others, or both.

I'm not a therapist, so I have no idea why a person behaves in a certain way. I'm just articulating a concept I've found to be true: when you know what your values are and you live in a way that reflects those values most of the time, you're going to be happy most of the time. If you live with a person who does not share your values, you will most likely not be happy. You will, in the most fundamental way, have nothing in common.

I've seen a lot of marriages. I've seen arranged marriages that work. I've seen love-at-first-sight marriages that work. I've seen marriages between interracial couples and gay couples. I've seen old men marry young women and vice versa. What I see most often in the enduring and happy marriages is that the partners share a lot of the same values.

So, what happens if you think something is important and your potential spouse feels exactly the opposite or doesn't prioritize that particular value? Or something is important to them and it's not important to you? That's when you have to decide *how* important it is to you or them. Is it a 'deal breaker'? Is it something that you can talk about, understand each other's perspectives, compromise without resentment, and move forward?

This is the work of marriage. The point of this book is to do this work now, before you're married or during your marriage, so you have less chance of marrying the wrong person or not understanding what's happening in your marriage when problems arise.

The most important aspect of communicating something that is important to you to your partner is to tell them very clearly how it (a particular behavior or situation) makes you feel. You also have to listen to your spouse about how your actions and certain situations make them feel. Then you have to decide how one or both of you is going to change your behavior.

If I repeat myself in this book, it's not because I've forgotten that I've said something. It's because I want you to remember it.

Questions to ask and answer

- What are your values? (Make a list.)
- How are these values expressed in your daily life? (Look at your calendar.)
- How are these values expressed in your daily habits? (Look at the quality of your life.)
- Are there values you say you have that you aren't fully living?
- What values do you see expressed in the daily life of your potential spouse?
- What values do you see expressed in the daily habits of your potential spouse?
- How do you spend your time?
- How does your potential spouse spend their time?
- Have you talked about money with your potential spouse?
- Have you discussed how you'll handle your money as a married couple?
- Have you talked about religion with your potential spouse?
- Do you share the same religion?
- Have you talked about children with your potential spouse?
- Have you discussed what you intend to teach your children?
- Have you discussed how you will discipline your children?
- Have you discussed what you expect of your children?
- Have you talked about politics with your potential spouse?
- Do you generally share the same political views?
- Have you talked about health with your potential spouse?

- Do the opinions and values you've heard expressed by your spouse during these conversations reflect the way they live their life?

- Do you and your potential spouse 'walk the walk' or just 'talk the talk' when it comes to values?

- Do you spend money shopping for non-essential items and then complain that you don't have any money?

- Do you forget or decline to vote and then complain about the state of the nation?

- Would you rather take pills to treat disease or exercise to preserve health?

- If your spouse told you that they were concerned about your health, would you take immediate and consistent steps to exercise and eat better?

Your Dating Experience

Your dating experience is critical to your marital experience for several reasons. First, it's your initial social interaction and emotional involvement with potential partners. Second, it provides a safe forum for you to explore your emotional world: what you are attracted to, physically and emotionally; what you need from a partner; and what you absolutely do not want or will not tolerate in a relationship.

What's more, you're going to discover what you can bring to a relationship. You're going to discover what other people need, what they want in a partner, and what their hopes and dreams are for the future. You'll do things together as you date potential partners, but, more importantly, you'll communicate with one another and explore how much you have in common and how different you are from each other. The things you have in common will be shared perspectives and experiences which will give you a sense of comfort and familiarity. The differences in opinions, tastes, skills, and personalities will provide balance, spark, and opportunities for personal growth.

The longer you date someone and the more exclusive your dating relationships become, the more these relationships resemble marriage. If you want to have a successful marriage, it would be helpful to have a successful dating experience.

Don't get me wrong: dating can and should be a lot of fun. You're meeting new people, getting to know them, having a great time, and experiencing that time in life where anything can happen and everything seems possible. The anticipation is awesome and the memories are magical. Enjoy it.

As delightfully dizzying as this dating period can be, however, it is also formative. Why? From the first moment you smile back at that gorgeous person at the table next to you, you are establishing how that person can, must, and should treat you. And they are letting you know, among other things, how you can, must, and should treat them.

This communication will continue for as long as the relationship continues. There will be verbal and nonverbal communications from the get-go that will tell every potential partner you meet how they can treat you in a relationship. The understanding and acceptance of a communication is an agreement. A relationship is a series of agreements.

Ladies, here are some questions to consider:

- ♥ Do the men you date open the door for you?

- ♥ Do they have to show up for a date dressed appropriately?

- ♥ Are they punctual? Or can they just 'hang out' with you whenever and 'see what happens'?

- ♥ Can they text you at 2 a.m. for, you know, a late night rendezvous that does not include dinner?

- ♥ Can they still see other women while you remain in an exclusive relationship with them?

Gentlemen, here are some questions for you:

- ♥ Do the women you date insist that you take them to an expensive restaurant or event every time you go out?

- ♥ Do they offer to pay after a couple of dates?

- ♥ Have they prepared a meal for you and invited you to dinner?

- ♥ Do they express their sincere appreciation for your time and effort by saying 'thank you' during and at the end of the date?

- ♥ Or can they just keep you hanging around while they date numerous other men, confident that you'll always be there?

Ladies, again:

- ♥ Do you dress like a hooker?
- ♥ Or do you dress like someone who requires respect?

Gentlemen:

- ♥ Are you treating her like a lady?
- ♥ Do either of you tolerate rudeness?
- ♥ Or are you both on your best behavior?
- ♥ Did you send or bring flowers?
- ♥ Did she send a thank you note for the flowers?

I've used pronouns for heterosexual relationships, but if you're gay or lesbian, I'm sure you understand what I'm saying.

To be clear, how you behave and how you allow other people to behave while dating will provide you and the world a fresh, clear picture of what you really think of yourself and how much you value yourself. The watchwords here are respect, courtesy, boundaries, and structure.

The boundaries and rules that you set up for yourself and the people who date you will define, to a large extent, the quality of your dating experience and the quality of the relationship that will probably, eventually, become your marriage.

The initial set of guidelines you experienced while dating may have been set by your parents. The reason that many parents establish strict rules for their sons' and daughters' dating experience is, to speak plainly, because they've been there and they know this stuff. They may not be able to articulate it as clearly as I do here (I'm a writer; that's my job), but they want to establish the 'rules of the game' for their child in order to protect them, physically and emotionally. They want the world to value their child the way they value their child, that is to say highly and with good reason. They also want to instill and communicate that sense of worth to their child, independent of their physical appearance or socio-economic background.

Hopefully, parents love and care for a child and raise the child to have a healthy set of values and a solid sense of self. But a child is a human being and, therefore, imperfect. A child is by definition immature. A child is susceptible to peer pressure and is likely to be insecure to some extent about a few things. As time passes, the child will grow up to be a young person and an adult. Some of these feelings of insecurity and inadequacy will fade. Some will remain.

You, as a young person, are well-advised to make this journey through life, insecurities and all, by using these guidelines, the 'rules of the game', that your family and society have set up for dating. These traditions have been created and maintained for a reason: they communicate value and boundaries to others. They show others that you value your time, your feelings, and your body. They convey boundaries regarding expected behavior. Through a deliberate and structured dating process, they also help you to become aware of, address, and negotiate your insecurities without making a big mistake and causing yourself and others a lot of pain.

Some of these rules include:

- ♥ How you and your date are expected to dress while on a date;
- ♥ How you and your date are expected to behave while on a date;
- ♥ What activities or events are permissible while on a date;
- ♥ What time a date is expected to end (the curfew).

Your parents may or may not be physically present to enforce rules of behavior on you or the people you date. Even if they are, you have to be responsible for yourself. You should understand that it's a bad idea to have sex with someone on the first date. You should understand that it's a bad idea to let your date drink and drive, or for you to drink and drive. You should understand that it's not acceptable for anyone to physically or emotionally abuse you or for you to abuse anyone else.

These three statements seem obvious, but your friends and dating partners may present arguments to the contrary that can, in the moment, make perfect sense. The thing I want to tell you is this: some of your friends and dating partners are idiots. Most of them, in fact, may be, especially those who propose sex on the first date, drinking and driving, or rationalizations for abuse. So don't listen to them. Listen to me.

The more a person is required to invest in something, whether it's an education, a business, or a relationship, the more they will value that same thing and the rewards and benefits they receive from it. I'm not saying that you need to behave like a diva. I'm saying you need to value yourself. If you don't value yourself, get down to the real reason you don't and address it, either by taking time to really think about your behavior or beliefs, talking it over with a friend, or getting professional help. That's your personal, interior, self-image work to be done alone and in private.

There are other things to be addressed in your social, public world.

- ♥ I strongly suggest that you first become aware and acknowledge that standards of behavior do exist.

- ♥ Second, your reputation in the dating world and the world in general will be created and maintained by your adherence to or disregard for these very same standards.

- ♥ Third, you are the only one to set those standards for yourself and your potential partners.

- ♥ Fourth, you need to articulate your standards clearly, first to yourself, and then to your partners, from the start of a relationship and all the way through it.

- ♥ Fifth, you're going to attract, relate to, and probably marry people who have the same standards as you do.

If you lower your standards enough, you can get married tomorrow, if that's what you think you want. If you raise and maintain your standards, over time you can attract potential partners who share your same high standards and have a chance a great dating experience and a great marriage.

I think you want to raise and maintain your standards and go for the good stuff over the long haul.

Note: during the dating process, and especially on college campuses, sadly, there is the danger of sexual assault, either from someone you're dating or socializing with, or from a stranger. Many times, these incidents happen when there is the excessive use of alcohol or drugs. Be smart. Upon arrival on a college campus, seek out information from classmates and university personnel about potentially dangerous events, parties, or groups. Avoid them.

If you want to consider yourself a gentleman, do not have sex or allow sex to happen if all parties involved cannot or do not consent. If you want to consider yourself a lady, keep a vigilant eye on your peers and your surroundings. Protect your friends. Moderate your alcohol intake. If a man can't or won't take 'No' for an answer, cause him as much physical pain as possible by kicking him in the genitals and scratching his face.

His skin under your fingernails gives you DNA evidence and will make it difficult for anyone to believe anything was consensual. It will also require your assailant to answer very uncomfortable questions from friends over the following days. Get to a safe place as quickly as possible. Call the police and file charges. Never, under any circumstances, speak to or date that person again.

Of course, the best way to avoid these problems is to establish and maintain dating standards that do not allow you to be put in an uncomfortable or dangerous situation to begin with.

Once you've established your own personal set of standards for yourself and for the people you'll consider dating, I would suggest that you give yourself a time frame. By this I mean that I would encourage you to date at least ten years before making a commitment to an exclusive relationship, engagement, or marriage.

This means if you start dating at age sixteen, you would be at least age twenty-six before you commit to someone, get engaged, or marry. Why would you want to set up a time frame for dating? The answer is time itself and the power it possesses. *Time is both a window and a mirror that can provide the opportunity for reflection, perspective, and clarity if you choose to use it properly.*

There is no substitute for time in the natural process of things, whether it is the nine months it takes to give birth to a baby, or the twelve months it takes for winter, spring, summer, and fall to come and go. You just can't rush things. And if you feel the urge to rush things, why do you want to rush things? What will change in a year or two if you are truly in love? The answer is nothing. Impatience, whether it be to make love, get married, or have children is indicative of some underlying issue that needs to be addressed. Find out what that issue is and address it before making a bad decision.

You want a substantial amount of time to date people. You want to date a variety of people, but I would suggest that you only date people that you would consider marrying. This may seem like a narrow-minded approach, but, trust me, after a while, guys get tired of buying dinners for girls who are just playing the field; girls get tired of guys who are just trying to find a sex partner for the evening. So let's just agree to be social, to a point, and then not waste anyone's time or money after that.

You will gain much wisdom and possess much awareness after you've been dating ten years. If you starting dating at age sixteen, by the age of twenty-six, you have a pretty good read on people you date. After three dates with the same person, you'll be able to determine if the relationship has a future. If it does, continue. If it doesn't, politely bow out.

The process of taking at least ten years to date, the wisdom you gain from it, and the personal growth you experience during it will help you strike a balance between enjoying yourself and finding the right person. You will grow and change a tremendous amount in ten years. What you want and need in a relationship will change, too. Allow for that.

During this period of nonexclusive dating, you may date people inside and outside your social class, people who have more and less education than you do, people who seem very much like you and very different than you. You'll be learning about them, but, most importantly, you'll be learning about yourself. You'll be learning what makes you happy, in the deep, long-term sense of the word. You'll also be discovering what you are and what you do that makes another person happy. You'll give yourself the opportunity to grow up and come into your own. You'll also give your potential partners that chance, too.

Note: if you are dating a woman and she mentions her 'biological clock' in conversation, that is a red flag. Run for the hills. If you're dating a man who uses the phrase 'my woman', that is a red flag. Run for the hills. Forcing deadlines on relationships is deadly. Being possessive of another person is toxic.

Absolutely avoid dating a married person. They will tell you ten different stories about their marriage and why they need your companionship, and some of these stories may even be true. If you really care about them, be patient with them. Let them get a divorce first. Let them have a year after their divorce is final to let the emotional (and probably financial) dust settle. Then consider dating them. Not until then. They may not appreciate your kind and patient reserve in the heat of the moment, but you will in the long run.

When you are dating another person non-exclusively, you will see how your potential partner respects your privacy as you date other people. You will see if they are unreasonably jealous or ridiculously competitive for your attention. You will see if their insecurities make them act out. You will see if they respect your judgment. You will see if they are patient with your decision-making process. You will see if they put pressure on you to date only them. You will see how they handle seeing you with another date in public. Can they manage their feelings?

And for all these things you may see in them, they may also have the chance to see all these things in you. Emotional pain is a two-way street, so I would encourage you, during this dating phase and in all phases of your relationships, to play fair and be kind. The worm turns, and your karma is all yours.

Your dating experience with another person should have balance. It should be mutually enjoyable. You should share serious ideas and concerns as well as joy and silliness. You should have an equal amount of interest in each other. The attraction should be mutual. It should also have structure and boundaries. It should be a process of slowly getting to know one another and gradually taking risks in sharing your feelings, hopes, and dreams with another person.

A patient dating strategy, with high standards of behavior for both parties involved, and with no premature commitments or expectations, allows a safe and open forum for emotions and communication to flow. Only laughter, tears, and memories hang in the balance. If you go through a few serious relationships in your high school, college, and young adult phases, and only have a few heartaches and a bunch of wonderful memories, you've done well.

There are dangers in not having standards, not dating for a long enough period of time, and not dating enough people. They run from the nagging regret, the feeling that you married too soon or didn't see enough of the world, to the life-altering bombs of sexually transmitted diseases, abuse, and unplanned pregnancy.

By defining and articulating your standards during your time dating and setting up a time frame, you do several things:

- ♥ You largely avoid physical and emotional dangers that can be life-altering;
- ♥ You enjoy the experience of dating;
- ♥ You learn about yourself as you go through the process;
- ♥ You give yourself a good chance to find the right partner without pressure.

Questions to Ask and Answer

- ♥ Were there standards of behavior communicated to you by your parents or family members regarding dating? If so, what were they?
- ♥ Do you feel like you generally accept or reject those standards?
- ♥ Have your peers or older siblings communicated their dating standards of behavior to you?
- ♥ Do you feel like you generally accept or reject those standards?
- ♥ Do you feel like it's acceptable to have sex with someone you've just met?
- ♥ Do you feel like it's acceptable to have sex with someone you know casually?
- ♥ Do you feel like it's acceptable to have sex with someone you know well and care for deeply?
- ♥ Do you feel like it's acceptable to have sex with someone you know well, care for deeply, and are in a committed, exclusive, long-term relationship with?
- ♥ Do you consistently date men who don't treat you with respect?
- ♥ Do you consistently date women who use you? Why?
- ♥ How do you dress for a date?
- ♥ How much preparation do you put into a date?
- ♥ Do you feel a sense of anticipation about a date?
- ♥ What do you want in a partner? (Make a list.)
- ♥ What do you need in a partner? (Add to the list.)
- ♥ What can you offer a partner?
- ♥ Do you date people that you would not consider marrying? Why?

Your First Commitment
Exclusivity

After you've dated for ten years, you probably have experienced several exclusive relationships that vary in their degrees of duration, intensity, and intimacy. You may have had a sweetheart in high school, a committed relationship in college, and a serious relationship as a young adult. Often, a relationship from high school or college extends into the next phase of life where it flourishes or dies, depending upon the geographic distance between partners, as well as the personal changes and emotional growth that the people involved go through.

I'm going to focus here on an adult relationship that occurs after college. It may have started in college, but it now involves two (fairly?) financially and emotionally self-sufficient young people who decide that they want to date each other exclusively. They're probably working for a living, or working and perhaps pursuing a post-graduate degree. Whatever the circumstances of their daily lives, the real world is fully present now. The days of giggling in the school cafeteria and singing silly songs in college are over.

It's at this point that you, as a young adult in this situation, may slowly or suddenly realize that you aren't going to live forever. You may also become aware that your options may not be fewer, but the choices that accompany them may be more important because the consequences of those choices become life-altering. You select a career. You interview for a job. Perhaps you move into an apartment and pay your own bills for the first time in your life. Maybe you do all this in a new city, far from home. Maybe your parents show signs of aging and you realize that one day you may have to take care of them.

On top of all these life changes, which can be exhilarating and exciting and wonderful, but also stressful, you've met someone who might be the person you want to spend the rest of your life with. You date for a period of time, and slowly the other people you were dating seem not so interesting. You let those relationships fade, or tell the also-rans that you've met someone else. It's important to note here that if only one of you has let all of his or her other relationships go and the other one is still dating around, someone is going to have to be patient. You can tell the person you're dating that they are the only person you're dating, but be ready for some hurt if they don't tell you the same thing.

Furthermore, you can't pressure someone into dating you exclusively. It has to be mutual and run a natural course. Ideally, you want to come to this realization at about the same time and articulate it to each other in an atmosphere of mutual understanding. There may even be an element of relief as a result of realizing that the only person you want to date only wants to date you. At a certain point in life, playing the field gets old.

The discussion of 'marriage' may not come up in this conversation and probably shouldn't, but being in sync (or not) with your partner on this first major point is going to be telling: you probably share the same values, but you also have to have a *simpatico* between you that is just as important, but more difficult to define. If you want to call this 'chemistry' or 'being on the same wavelength' with one another, that's fine.

Here are some characteristics of a good match at this point in your relationship:

- ♥ You're both comfortable with dating each other exclusively;
- ♥ You both reached this realization at about the same time;
- ♥ It was probably understood by both of you without being articulated;
- ♥ You're both very excited about it.

So, over a pizza or a cup of coffee or a candlelit dinner, you and your partner finally discuss the subject of dating each other exclusively. You agree, probably with warm smiles that spill into nervous laughter, to take this step.

This is the first important moment for you and your potential partner. Why? Because you're risking together, with agreed upon terms, with a shared intention of seeing if this relationship is going to work. And by work, I mean that you think this person is going to be someone that fulfills your needs. They also 'float your boat' emotionally with a great deal of joy and understanding. They are the person that you are going to want to be next to as you work to accomplish individual and shared goals, enjoy or endure life's experiences, perhaps have and raise children, and comfort in old age and in death. So this is a little bit of a big deal. You should be nervous. You should think it through carefully. And when you have, you should feel confident that you and your partner can take this first step together.

You're excluding other people you've met — and haven't met — in the belief that no one you're ever going to meet is going to be as interesting, caring, and perfect of a companion. This is the person that you think, hope, believe, or at least suspect, might be The One.

The critical aspects of this first commitment is that you aren't going to date, have sex with, or get romantically involved with anyone else. It's just one commitment, one thing. And that's a good thing. Why? *Because you can't handle more than one thing right now.* You can't handle setting up house together and sharing financial responsibilities, raising children, and dealing with life 24/7.

You can't handle it as a couple because you haven't known each other long enough. You probably can't handle it individually because you haven't been self-sufficient long enough. You probably don't have the emotional resources and you may not have the financial resources. And if, by chance, you do have them at the start of the relationship, you may not have them at the end, which could come sooner than you would want.

So be happy and grateful that you only have one commitment in your relationship to honor at this point. And make no mistake: it's a big one that you will promise to honor right now, and for the rest of your life if you marry this person.

I'll venture a couple of predictions of what you could experience during this period of exclusivity: first, you or your partner may meet someone else who absolutely turns your world upside down. This encounter will make you completely doubt yourself and your existing relationship, and throw the best laid plans into the air. How far you or your partner let this go, no one knows. How much damage it does, no one knows. How this turns out, no one knows.

The realization that this was just an infatuation may come to light before things have gone too far. The realization that your existing relationship is lacking in some key emotional issue (for you or your partner) may come to light and need to be addressed. Or there may be the realization that one of you is not as good as they could be in honoring the one single commitment you made to each other. And you'll have to face that, individually and as a couple.

The sizzle may fizzle, too. That anticipation that you initially felt in seeing your partner may fade as a certain amount of routine sets in. Dates may not be the big productions they were at the outset. No one is trying to impress anyone. You're still going out, still having fun, but the excitement and interest just doesn't last.

Or you could just move forward, learning more about each other, falling more deeply in love, and becoming more of a couple than you ever thought possible.

I'll also offer some specific advice: don't make any grand announcements or pronouncements to friends and family about the fact that you're dating each other exclusively. They know you. They can tell you're probably in love. If some of the clueless or malicious offer to set you up on a date with someone else, politely decline. This is a time to keep this private, if not exactly secret.

Sure, you're proud of your new love. You want to show them off to the world. However, more importantly, you want to continue to nurture this person and learn about this relationship without external pressure, without social expectations, without other people's agendas. You also want to be able to have this relationship fail without enduring unnecessary public scrutiny as well as personal pain.

This is a key thing to understand about your relationship: it's about you and your partner and how you're progressing. It's about how things are when you are completely alone with your partner. It's not about anyone or anything else. This relationship is young. It needs protection from the elements. There will be plenty of time, later on, to expose it to the fair and foul winds of friends, family, career, and the world at large.

So keep it low-key, keep it private, and keep it personal. Take baby steps.

Questions to Ask and Answer

- ♥ How many exclusive relationships have you been in?
- ♥ How long did each last?
- ♥ What caused the end of each relationship?
- ♥ Are you in an exclusive relationship now?
- ♥ Did you both mutually agree on this arrangement at about the same time?
- ♥ Is it similar to or different from your previous exclusive relationships?
- ♥ In what ways is it unique?
- ♥ What did you learn from each relationship?
- ♥ Are you a different person now than you were during your first exclusive relationship?
- ♥ Have you betrayed the trust of your partner by cheating in an exclusive relationship?
- ♥ How did that turn out?
- ♥ Have you been cheated on?
- ♥ Do you see similarities in the partners you choose?
- ♥ How long do you think you should be in an exclusive relationship before becoming engaged?

Your Second Commitment
Engagement

You've been dating exclusively for a year or longer. You've walked in the moonlight, watched the sun come up together, fought and made up, shared your life stories, met the parents, visited each other's hometowns and old neighborhoods, and grown together as a couple and, certainly, as individuals. You love each other in a solid, confident way. You're certain that you're ready for marriage. You're not.

You may be ready to be *engaged to be married*. Being engaged to be married differs in a few subtle but important ways from simply dating each other exclusively.

First, it's definitive. Someone has asked someone to marry them and the other someone has agreed to marry. It's one of the most joyful moments in your life. Cherish the memory. My sincere wish is that you experience it only once and have a lifetime of great love and life to follow.

Your relationship changes with this second commitment. The permanence of your relationship and the level of risk and trust increases. Your behavior and your choices from this point forward impact not only you, but the one you care most about. Oh, and now, it impacts your family, and their family, and all of your friends.

The second way being engaged is different is that it's usually public. Everybody knows. Everybody's happy for you. Your success or failure as a couple will be, from this point forward, common knowledge by those in both your families and your social circle.

Before we continue, let me say this: being an Old Money Guy (as well as the originator of the term), I discourage couples from purchasing an engagement ring. I think it's a waste of money. I think it's a retail racket. Actually, I know it is. The idea that you, as a man, must buy a woman an engagement ring to give her when you propose marriage was invented by a marketing firm about 75 years ago. Americans accept it as a tradition now, an obligation that they must somehow honor, even if they can't afford it. The most recent spin on this marketing campaign was the formula that the groom should save up and then spend three months' salary on the wedding ring for his bride.

Set yourself free from that foolishness. This is something that, as a married couple, you're going to have to learn to do: ignore what the rest of the world says you should do, and do what's right for you. The best place to start is to not pay retail for a diamond ring to show the rest of the world (allegedly) how much money you have or how much you love someone.

Relationships are not about the diamond ring that you can show off to your girlfriends. Grow up. You may want to present to or share with the one you love some token of your love. That's understandable. However, if your intention is to start a life together being honest and responsible—"Honestly, I think we would be better off saving money than buying jewelry"—then you need to have a serious talk with your partner prior to somebody going off the deep end at the local jewelry store.

You'll notice I used the term 'we' in the previous paragraph. That's what being engaged changes. It changes your point of reference. It is now 'we' on all major decisions and most of the minor ones. So if you feel like your fairy tale proposal just wouldn't be complete without a five-carat solitaire that your Prince Charming presents you on bended knee at the foot of the Eiffel Tower, I need you to wake up and smell the coffee.

If your fiancé is rich and money is no object, let your imagination and his credit card run wild. But if you are on any kind of a budget, or Old Money, in your heart you know better. This is the place where you start making financial decisions together. You're either the one who's going to buy the ring or the one who's going to accept it.

I see it not as an expression of love, but a major purchase made by one partner without consulting the other. I'm not cold or lacking in the romance department at all, but I am practical about important things. And this is important. It involves money, the start of your life together, your decision making process about big expenditures, and it shapes your future.

Guys, if you must buy her a ring, buy her a wedding ring on a gold chain that she can wear around her neck until your wedding day. Then you can take the ring off her chain and put it on her finger. Make it a simple gold or platinum band. Skip the diamonds. If you must buy diamonds, look at estate pieces. You get more for your money than buying a brand new diamond ring.

And guys, don't propose in a public place and make a big production out of it. You're going to have to put your ego on a shelf or in a drawer once you get married. You might as well start now. This isn't about anyone else seeing how clever or romantic you can be. It also puts a lot of pressure on the person you're proposing to.

Girls, I know it's important for a guy to express his feelings for you. Just let him off the hook with this engagement ring nonsense. Think about, discuss, and plan your future together. The first big financial dent you can avoid in your relationship is the expense of an engagement ring. So avoid it.

I've seen some of the wealthiest women in the world wearing a simple gold band as a wedding ring. Not surprisingly, they are also the ones who have been married to the same man for the longest. Why? Because the simplicity of the wedding ring probably symbolizes that the relationship is about the commitment, not the show.

Now, let's get back to the business of being engaged. Depending on your personal preferences, culture, and traditions, you'll probably inform your respective parents about your decision to marry shortly before or after the proposal. You're both wading into deeper waters now: other people are involved.

A dinner with the newly engaged couple and the future in-laws is a likely result. This will bring to the front the next step you'll take as an engaged couple: The Plan. Most parents are happy to hear that their child is planning to get married. It's a joyful moment. There are usually tears (of joy) and heartfelt embraces. A new family is being born, and existing families are growing.

You want to bolster that joy by adding a sense of comfort. This is done by presenting your respective sets of parents with The Plan. The timeframe for this plan began when one of you proposed marriage and the other accepted, and perhaps prior to that. It extends to the wedding day and beyond.

The Plan is a timetable you and your partner will conceive at first in broad terms, and then in detail. It will be in writing, not just in your head. It will calendar how you're going to progress as a couple prior to marriage, how you're going to plan your wedding, when and perhaps where you're going to have your wedding, and how you're going to plan your life together, as far as you can reasonably see into the future. It will include a savings plan. Money may be kept in separate checking or savings accounts prior to the wedding (I recommend this.) But the intention is that the assets will be joined together when you are married.

The Plan includes who is going to work at what job for how long and where. Which religion or church denomination you're going to belong to and how devoutly you're going to practice that religion, if any. If one of you is still trying to break into a career or going to grad school, you'll detail what compromises you're both going to make, and for how long, until things change for the better. It includes what changes will occur in health care coverage, life insurance, and estate planning (wills, trusts, etc.) once you are married.

It is very important that both of you draft valid wills which, depending upon where you live, should probably be signed in the presence of a notary and notarized. Also consider advance health care directives, which detail your wishes in a medical emergency or in the face of long-term care. There are numerous resources online that offer information and insight about these issues. There are also attorneys that specialize in this area.

What your estate planning needs actually are at the time you marry depends on the amount of your estate, your particular family situation, your profession, and your personal preferences. Doing these things may cost money or may not, but do not neglect them. The Plan may include agreements about children and who is responsible for birth control. You may want to select a family doctor and a family attorney for the new family. Sit down, grab a pencil and paper, get comfortable, and make The Plan. It may take thirty minutes. It may take three weeks. Do it.

As a couple, you will then decide how much of this you share with your in-laws and extended family and how much advice on these matters you want to solicit from them. I suggest you keep your financial affairs private for your entire lives together. Start now. Share with your parents your career plans and where and how you want to live. Give them as clear a picture as you can. But your money is your business.

You may also want to discuss a prenuptial agreement if you feel that is necessary. (Note: couples who do not pool their money when they get married are 145% more likely to get divorced.) I've heard more than one person say that if you need a 'prenup' you're doing at least one of three things:

- ♥ Marrying outside your social class;
- ♥ Marrying someone who does not share your values; and/or
- ♥ Headed for trouble.

I've heard this from Old Money Guys and Gals, as well as newly-minted millionaires with plenty to lose in a marriage. I do see the other side of the argument when you or your partner look at the preservation of wealth accumulated over generations. I wish you all the luck in the world if you have to have that conversation. Many relationships do not survive it.

The Plan should address the size, cost, and logistics (geographical and interpersonal) of the wedding. Let me say this clearly: your wedding is your wedding. It is important to set boundaries for involvement in your affairs now, as an engaged couple. Your engagement and its terms as laid out in The Plan are the first set of boundaries for other people. The Plan shows everybody that you've discussed it, thought it through, and you are now communicating it.

You establish your second set of boundaries as you plan your wedding. How much and in what way you allow others to inject their wishes into your engagement and wedding may color your relations with your extended family for years to come. Be polite. Be flexible. Be united. Be firm. Debate and decide all this before you present The Plan to The Parents. If issues come up in conversation, don't make a decision on the spot unless you are both in immediate and obvious agreement. Discuss it later in private if you're not sure about something or if you're inclined to disagree.

You want to be inclusive when you present The Plan. If your parents have had a good marriage, you can learn from them. Start now. Ask for any words of wisdom. They'll appreciate the gesture, even if they only respond with vague platitudes about forgiveness and acceptance. You also want to keep it light. This may be a tense moment. Don't be reluctant to laugh about any awkwardness you may be feeling. Finally, you want to be united when you present The Plan to The Parents. You're not laying down the law, but you are drawing a polite line in the sand. The Plan may (and most likely will) change, but at least you have one.

The main points you want to cover are:

- ♥ The length of the engagement,
- ♥ The approximate date, location, and size of the wedding;
- ♥ Where you're going to live when you get married;
- ♥ What career plans you have as you start your life together; and
- ♥ When or if children fit into the picture.

Unless you elope, you will have to negotiate the details of the wedding and how involved your families become in planning or paying for that. (More on the subject later.)

Note: I suggest that you do not live together prior to getting married. If you want to live together, live together. Work out your own rules regarding responsibilities, finances, and loyalties and cohabitate. Many people are happy living together. Many people are happy being married. Mixing the two concepts is tricky business because simply living together is usually a very fluid arrangement that can be terminated easily and quickly. If there are no children involved, one person just moves out.

Marriage, on the other hand, is a very structured arrangement that many times requires thought, preparation, and expense to enter into and, as we all know, to get out of. These are two very different social and emotional arrangements that, in my opinion, reflect two very different mindsets. If you want one, you probably don't want the other. The level of commitment is just too different. It muddies the water. Avoid it.

I also suggest that you be engaged to each other a minimum of two years prior to getting married. Why? First, this is going to be the public debut of your relationship. This change will bring elements of attempted influence and perhaps turbulence. The most common example of this influence may be a mother-in-law (or two) who want to plan every detail of the wedding, as I mentioned. A second, more welcome, example may be a generous in-law who wants to contribute to your future together by offering one of you a position in his company or offering to give you money. (This sounds like a dream come true, but these offers rarely come with 'no strings attached.' Beware.)

You and your partner both want to see and hope for the best in people, especially in the people you love. But people are human beings and when they see a change in their relationship with someone they love, like their child or sibling, they may behave strangely, even without realizing it. And someone getting married is a big change in a relationship, no matter how close you are. Family members and friends may feel like they're losing you. To a certain extent, they are. Be understanding. Be compassionate.

The reality is that your loyalty now resides with your partner, not your mother, father, brother, sister, or best friend. That's the next big difference in your life. That's another reason why I suggest you have at least a two year engagement. Give yourself, your partner, family, and friends time to adjust.

The process for you and your partner is to gradually blend your two lives together. Your lives include your careers, your social circles, your present daily routines, as well as your distant hopes and dreams. You will also want to let some 'water go under the bridge', so to speak. In any given two year period, you will experience triumphs and disappointments, surprises and shocks.

In the past, you faced these alone or with your family and friends. Now you share them with your partner. You will be the primary emotional support for them, and they for you. This is going to be new, exciting, and challenging, whether it's a big promotion at work or the loss of a close friend or family member.

Another aspect of this is the adjustment period you need as you both assimilate into your partner's family. If you live in the same area as your future in-laws, there is the presumption that you will be spending some time together. If you don't, you could at least be expected to share holiday time together. This is easier if you and your partner have the same socio-economic backgrounds or share the same culture, pasttimes, or traditions. Even then, it's work. You both need the time to learn how each other's families function and to find your respective places within each. This is also true of the groups of friends you share or individually bring to the relationship.

Give yourself and your partner time to adjust, to learn, and to grow into these new roles. As conflicts and revelations present themselves, you'll have the opportunity to communicate your feelings with each other, make adjustments and compromises, and reach a new level of emotional intimacy. You'll also have the chance to laugh hysterically, love with abandon, and embrace your new extended family.

Questions to Ask and Answer

- ♥ Do you know how your partner feels about the purchase of an engagement ring?
- ♥ Are you or your partner in a rush to get married?
- ♥ If you are in a rush to get married, why are you in a rush?
- ♥ Have you and your partner discussed or written down The Plan for the next few years?
- ♥ Have you or your partner discussed a prenuptial agreement?
- ♥ How did this make you feel?
- ♥ How well do you get along with your partner's family?
- ♥ Are you financially prepared to be married right now?
- ♥ Will you be more prepared in two years?
- ♥ Have you already experienced your partner enduring a painful loss or disappointment?
- ♥ How did you support them?
- ♥ If you experienced a recent success or financial windfall, did you consider it your success?
- ♥ Did you consider it a success for you and your partner?
- ♥ Did you celebrate it as your success or your shared success as a couple?

Your Biggest Commitment
Marriage

Before we dive in to a discussion of marriage, let's recap the road map that I've laid out here. If you've followed my advice, you've dated for a decade or so. You've dated a variety of people, but the people that you've dated for extended periods of time have been people within your social class or closely in its range. You've primarily dated people that you would consider potential marriage partners. You dated people who had a lot in common with you: they shared your values.

You've avoided unhealthy relationships by moving slowly in the dating process and making sure there was always mutual respect between you and the people you dated. You've avoided people who were too possessive. You've avoided people whose ambitions and direction in life didn't really match your own. You've avoided people with substance abuse issues.

You've introduced a couple of your potential partners to family and friends. They shot down one of them, and you realized they were right. But the second person you brought home was a winner. You dated for another year, exclusively. A few months later, a proposal was made and accepted. You were on top of the world and still are.

A two year engagement followed that. During this time, you were still giggling in cafes and taking long walks in the park, but the business of life edged its way into your lives. You talked through and came up with The Plan. You've had a few surprises (mostly good) as a couple. You've both become comfortable with each other's families, and they've become comfortable with you. You've had the time to get your financial house in order. You're ready to take care of each other.

You set an approximate date for the wedding a couple of years ago. As time passed, the date became firmer and closer. Now, it's here. You're going to be married to the person you love. You've known them for at least four years and have probably dated them exclusively for three years, two of those years being engaged.

You had a feeling that they were The One, but you're very glad that you went through a period of time with them prior to marriage. Time gave you the opportunity to get to know each other without pressure. It gave you the chance to develop skills and processes to handle disagreements and iron out personal wrinkles that were impacting your relationship. You learned to reach compromises and accept shortcomings. You bonded through a couple of bad times and jumped for joy during several high points. It gave you the chance to be certain that this was the person you wanted to go through the rest of your life together with. You grew up as you grew together.

Now, The Big Day approaches. It's probably the biggest day of your life. You know this. But let me tell you why this is the biggest day of your life.

I'll start with a brief history of the institution of marriage. Marriage was originally simply a way to preserve wealth and pass it along to the next generation in an orderly fashion. Love had very little to do with it. Families within a shared social class subtly (or brazenly) steered their children into suitable or profitable matches for mutual benefit. A dowry, a lump sum of money or property that accompanied the bride on the wedding day, was usually a part of the arrangement.

Marriage was also a social construct to keep order in society. It proved to be a productive way to have and raise children. Throughout history, of course, love has entered the equation to varying degrees. Today, most people marry someone they truly love.

Still, I think it's unwise to ignore the origins of an institution. They still have relevance for us today. First, I think 'marrying for love' alone is very dangerous. You can be 'in love' with someone and then fall out of love with them. Some scientists have proposed the theory that romantic love is actually a chemical reaction in the bodies of two people that lasts about eighteen months then subsides.

Whatever the truth, it's fair to say that romance comes and goes for varying periods of time in all marriages. You still love the person, even if you're not hearing violins every day of the year. However, if you don't have anything in common with them, being married to them when you are not 'in love' with them (whether it's for a moment or a year) is going to be very unpleasant. This may be why the divorce rate is so high.

Many married people, or those about to be married, don't realize or acknowledge that their love is going to grow and evolve over time. They may think they understand it, but many of them deny it or are blinded by the halo that shines around their beloved's head. Romance is great, but you've got to have more going for your relationship than that.

Furthermore, it's unfair to any children a marriage might produce if the two partners involved have not thoroughly understood what marriage is. There needs to be a lot of homework and just plain work done to make it a success. And it's the adults' job to do it. Children don't ask to be born, as far as we know. (Wink, nod.) They simply come into the world and need to be loved. A broken or dysfunctional home is no good for anyone.

The deliberate and practical approach to dating and marriage I present in this book may strike you as fatiguing to read, consider, and execute. It is not, however, half as exhausting as being in a bad marriage. This book may seem calculated and even cynical. It is not. However, this book is free of the bitterness you find in many people after a nasty divorce. If you have chosen the right person, working through the steps and processes in this book will not ruin your relationship. It will enhance it. If you have not chosen the right person, this book may bring that to light and save you both a lot of pain.

The reason you have to put a lot of thought into marrying the right person is because you still bring a dowry, something of tremendous value, to the marriage on your wedding day. You are giving that to the person you love. It's a risk, and you should be aware of it.

You have love. You have a heart. You have dreams, goals, desires, faults, and fears. You have this one life. Time only moves forward. You cannot press a reset button and delete a mistake or relive a memory. You will not live forever. Your life is precious and has value.

You have secured an education and gained wisdom that you can share with the world. You have an opportunity as you get married, not to only double your opportunities in life, but to increase them exponentially. You have, together and individually, social contributions that you can and should make to the world and a legacy that you can leave long after you're gone.

These things are your dowry, whether you are a woman or a man about to get married. You trust the person you marry to cherish, treasure, protect, preserve, and nurture this dowry. And let's not pretend: there may be money, too. If you choose the wrong person to marry, you may lose a substantial portion of your wealth. This is why I emphasize only dating people who share your values, social class, and ambitions.

If you marry someone who does not share your values, you may lose time: months or years in an unhappy marriage that, unlike money, you cannot recoup. You may have your heart broken, an event from which you may or may not fully recover. You may also have children with this person, and the suffering will be shared not only by you and your spouse, but by innocent young people who did nothing to deserve it and are not equipped to handle it.

People, usually parents, throughout the centuries have understood the unpleasant realities I've just articulated to you. That's why they have wanted to play a determining role regarding who and when their children marry.

So, yes, this is a big deal.

As you prepare for The Big Day, you and your partner begin to plan your wedding.

I recommend that you have a small, simple, and inexpensive wedding. As I've noted in "The Old Money Book," the average wedding in America just a couple of years ago costs $30,000. That's a lot of money in this age of stagnant wages, falling home prices, and tenuous employment.

Let me offer some additional thoughts. If your parents have the money to pay for your wedding, they also have the option of setting that lump of cash in a trust fund and designating it for the education, care, and future well-being of any child or children you and your new spouse may have.

They could also offer it as a down payment on a piece of real estate at an appropriate time in the future (not immediately.) Or they could simply wait and give you and your new spouse the cash as a five year anniversary present. Any scenario, other than spending it on a one day event, would offer you and your spouse an advantage in the future.

If you choose to spend $30,000 or $50,000 or $100,000 on a wedding, you should realize that you or your parents will have that money on one day, and the next day, after your wedding, that money will be gone. You should be very aware of what you are getting for that amount of money. Is it memories? Is it social status? Is it your 'fairy tale' wedding? You should also calculate how quickly you can make and save that amount of money again.

If you or your spouse made a million bucks last year, drop a hundred big ones on the big day. You'll make in back in a month. No big deal. If you, or the people paying for the wedding, made only $100,000 last year, I'd question your sanity and judgment in spending, or letting someone else spend, that much on any event. It will take you years to recoup it. You may never recoup it. And if you need it and don't have it, you may resent the person or people who decided to spend it.

If you make an emotional decision instead of a logical decision regarding the cost of your wedding, you will be making surely the first and perhaps biggest financial mistake of your married life. Why? Because money problems are one of the biggest problems in marriage. Do everything you can to avoid them. If you can save a huge lump sum on your wedding and hold on to it, whether it's in your bank account or your parents', it doesn't matter. You'll be much better off, financially and emotionally.

Second, you need to remember that your wedding is about you and your spouse, nobody else. If it happens in your uncle's backyard with twenty guests or at St. Paul's in Manhattan with three thousand in attendance, you will still be married just the same. You will stand no better chance of being happy. You will still remember the day forever. The only difference will be that you, or your parents, will still have the money. Or not.

Another reason to have a simple wedding is to avoid stress. This is the biggest day of your life so far. Keep it simple. Manage it. Enjoy it.

Now, you've decided where, when, and how to have the wedding. It is the day of the wedding. I will tell you this: if, immediately prior to your wedding, you have reservations or trepidation about getting married, do not do it. That feeling is your instinct telling you not to do it, and you should listen to it.

If, however, you have heeded my advice in this book, you'll probably be very confident, somewhat relaxed, a little nervous, and truly excited about your new life together. You've taken your time with this process. You've thought it through yourself. You've talked it through as a couple. And now you're doing it together.

At this point, you might expect a detailed list or long dissertation about what to do and how to act toward your new partner now that you're married. But you've already learned that. You established those rules of kindness, mutual respect, and fair play from the first moment you interacted with each other. Certainly they were communicated and understood in the first few dates.

What changes when you are married is your legal status in society. It is a matter of public record. It has financial consequences. If you are financially irresponsible and go too far into debt, both you and your spouse may have to declare bankruptcy. If the police break down your front door and find a kilo of cocaine in the bathroom, and you honestly knew nothing about it, you may still go to prison for possession.

Your behavior now directly impacts your spouse. Your spouse's behavior directly impacts you. Your behavior must now be, at all times, completely above board. Secrets between married people are best few and far between, and of little consequence. If you make a mistake, you want to be in a marriage where you feel comfortable, if not happy, to admit it and try to fix it. If your spouse admits a mistake, you should be the kind of person who can address it and forgive it without resentment, whether it's a bathtub that overflowed or a car that's been totaled.

Ultimatums, threats, and revenge have no place in a marriage. Hurtful sarcasm or 'talking out of school' to friends or relatives about the intimate details of your marriage, or problems within your marriage, is a nonstarter.

If you've done it right, you already know that you can go to your spouse when you've screwed up, confess, and be okay. This comfort and trust has been built up over time, without the pressure of being married, when each party was free to walk away. Now that each party is not as free to walk away, it's alright: precedents have been established. The foundation has been laid. Life can go on.

They say every marriage is a foreign country, with its own customs, traditions, celebrations, and taboos. Your marriage will have its own unique characteristics, but the most common basic rules of a marriage are:

- ♥ Not to cheat on the other person;
- ♥ Not to lie to them;
- ♥ To never physically hurt them; and
- ♥ To never intentionally hurt them emotionally.

If one of you is having a difficult time, the other should pick up the slack until they're back to their normal self. You should support one another in good times and bad. You should care for one another. And, of course, you should love each other.

I'm going to offer some additional concepts that you can feel free to consider.

If someone is your friend, they don't have to necessarily be your spouse's friend. But if someone is the enemy of one of you, they are now the enemy of both of you.

If someone asks you not to tell your spouse something, you must decide how your spouse will feel if they find out that you kept this secret from them. If it's no big deal, don't tell your spouse. If it's a big deal, or if you're in doubt, tell your spouse.

You don't keep health issues secret from your spouse.

You don't discuss health issues outside your marriage unless both of you agree to do so.

If a friend of your spouse makes an inappropriate comment or move toward you, tell your spouse and rightfully expect that their friendship is over.

Questions to Ask and Answer

- Do you absolutely need a huge, expensive, and very public wedding? Why?
- Can you afford the wedding you're planning?
- Do you feel pressure from friends or family to have a more elaborate wedding than you would prefer?
- Do you feel a social obligation to have a big wedding? Why?
- Do you feel that a big wedding will convey some social benefit?
- What would that be?
- Are you and your spouse in agreement with how much involvement your in-laws and family members will have with your wedding ceremony?
- Do you feel like your relationship is going to change a great deal when you marry?
- Do you feel like it's going to be a transition, but not that big of a change?
- Do you feel like it's not going to change at all?
- Do your wedding plans take into consideration both sides of the family equally?
- Do your wedding plans create any hardships for people in the wedding party in terms of travel, inconvenience, or expense?
- Have you been contacted by a wedding planner?
- If so, did the wedding planner exert any undue pressure on you?
- Did the wedding planner sit down with you and your spouse? Or just you?
- Did you make any commitments verbally, financially, or in writing to a wedding planner without the knowledge and consent of your spouse?

Your Expectations

Your marriage is a combination of unspoken and verbal agreements, as well as a set of expectations regarding your behavior and the behavior of your spouse. Don't be under any illusions. You have committed your life to another person, and they've committed their life to you. Performance is required.

By that I mean you're expected to do everything you can do to make your marriage a success. Your spouse expects this. Your family expects this. Society expects this. In the Bible there's a verse that reads something like, 'Faith without works is dead.' I'd paraphrase that and say, 'Love without effort is not going to live long.'

You have to show the person you married that you love them and put them first in your life. They must, in turn, do that for you. This reciprocal, equal, and consistent state of prioritizing the other person is the key to a vibrant marriage. I'm not talking about fawning women being subservient to macho men, or mousey men being hen-pecked by overbearing women. I'm talking about a commitment to always think about your spouse first. This is the expectation that you must have of yourself and of your spouse.

There is an irony to this way of thinking and acting: the attention and effort that go out toward your partner will nourish and fulfill you emotionally as they, feeling fulfilled, loved, and joyful, give back to you. And the opposite is true: if you're always thinking about taking care of yourself first, your partner will feel neglected, and your marriage will suffer.

This commitment to think this way and act this way requires a substantial amount of love and trust. It doesn't mean that you never say, 'I really feel this way about this subject,' or 'I really want to do this.' Your individuality doesn't disappear when you get married, but some of your selfishness and self-centered needs are going to have to take a back seat for the good of the team.

I know of one couple who have been happily married for an extended period. The wife is a devout Christian and attends church every Sunday. I mean every Sunday. Her husband is certain that God exists, but he is less certain that any religious building or doctrine confers exclusive access to the Almighty or His blessings. Nevertheless, he attends church with her regularly. What he's thinking during the sermon, I have no idea, but he does remain conscious and gives every appearance of being attentive to, if not engrossed in, the proceedings.

We discussed these differences in beliefs and practices between his wife and him. When asked why he goes to church with her, he simply shrugged and said, 'She's happier when we go together.' It was a brief response that spoke volumes. He acquiesced to her wishes regarding this particular thing. I'm sure that she has compromised and blessed him with her presence (or absence) during activities that he enjoys.

Here are some concepts to remember:

- ♥ You give first.
- ♥ You receive in return.
- ♥ You give more than you take.
- ♥ You think of your spouse before you speak.
- ♥ You think of your spouse before you act.
- ♥ You do not keep score.
- ♥ You do maintain balance.
- ♥ You listen to your spouse's feelings and opinions.

- ♥ You share your feelings and opinions.
- ♥ You work it out.
- ♥ You reach an accord.
- ♥ You honor the agreement.
- ♥ You forget the disagreement.

The agreement in question can be something as small as who does the dishes on Monday, Wednesday, and Friday or as big as who will put their career on hold for a year while a family crisis is resolved. If for some reason, you feel that you are unable to honor an agreement that you and your spouse have made, or you see that they are not honoring an agreement, you need to discuss it.

By discuss it, I don't mean accuse your spouse of failure. Nor do I mean to beat yourself up because you thought you could do something and now it seems you can't. I mean talk about it gently, honestly, and in private. From that point, you communicate, listen, understand, get to the bottom of it, and reach another agreement.

Another saying that you will hear intelligent married men say is, 'Happy wife…happy life.' This is the wisdom of a man who through experience understands that prioritizing his wife's happiness and addressing her concerns usually means that she makes his life just as enjoyable, if not more so. It also reflects a set of values that place the marriage at the front of the line in terms of importance. It is indicative of an individual who measures his self-esteem by the quality, nature, and duration of his commitments to his partner. He has set his ego aside and taken hold of a greater purpose.

To be sure, you cannot *make* another person happy. You can, however, endeavor to fulfill their needs, understand their desires, contribute to their well-being, share important moments with them, and help them accomplish their goals. Somehow, some way, it seems that a large measure of mutual happiness often results from sincerely and consistently making an effort in these areas.

That's just been my experience.

Questions to Ask and Answer

- What expectations do you have as you enter your marriage?
- What expectations does your spouse have?
- How do you plan to act, individually and as a couple, in order to fulfill those expectations?
- What compromises have you already made in order to facilitate happiness in your relationship?
- Do you feel any resentment at having made those concessions? Why?
- Can you let go of those resentments?
- Are you consistently giving more than you're receiving in your relationship?
- Do you feel the same can be said of your partner?
- Are you receiving an adequate amount of emotional support from your partner?
- Have you discussed any imbalance or unfairness you feel exists in your relationship?
- Have you worked out a new agreement based on that discussion?
- Are new actions being taken by you and your partner to honor the agreement?
- Do you often make commitments to your partner that you do not honor? Why?

Your Mutual Understandings

To a large extent, your mutual understandings as a married couple are going to have their origins in the culture, beliefs, background, values, educational experience, and social class that you each have absorbed and embraced in your lifetime and have brought with you to the marriage. These understandings will merge and evolve over the course of your marriage, but, once again, you should both share many of these at the start.

The reason you need to have a grasp on this concept is simple: the more mutual understandings you have at the start of your marriage, the fewer discussions and disagreements you'll have about certain issues. The fewer disagreements you'll have about how you're going to handle, for example, money and raising children, the more likely it is that you'll be happy and have plenty of energy to handle other issues that arise.

These understandings might be simply called, 'the things you have in common', but it's important to articulate them a little more clearly and connect with them on a deeper level. These shared values, ideals, and everyday assumptions that you and your spouse both make will form the foundation of your relationship and help it endure difficult times. It is also a base upon which you can expand and enrich your relationship.

Once again, I'm going to encourage you to write these down and really *appreciate them*. Your relationship may have sparked over small things. Perhaps you both enjoy Charles Dickens' novels. It may have sizzled over your differences. Perhaps you have a love/hate relationship with those crazy madras pants he wears with his blue blazer. But it will survive and flourish because of your mutual understandings.

These mutual understandings are not written in stone, nor do they exist in a bubble. They have been adopted early by you and are substantial, but can they also change slowly over time. One of the places that these mutual understandings are first recognized, articulated, and shared is in college. As diverse as a college campus can appear, the people on campus have fundamental beliefs in common: first, they (or their parents) believe that a college education is important; second, they believe that they will benefit from it; third, they believe they will enjoy it.

These are basic concepts, but they provide the individuals who comprise the student body a set of fundamental shared values. During the four-year college experience, beliefs are identified, confirmed or rejected, revised, expanded, and embraced for the long haul. Students are in an environment where they share experiences, often challenging ones. They bond in groups—fraternities, sororities, or clubs focusing on curriculum or career interests.

They also bond romantically as couples. This most often happens when the mutual understandings of two people are recognized and appreciated by each other. You have enough in common to relate with each other and enough differences to be interesting and helpful to each other. Logistically, couples are in the same location for an extended period of time and often independent of their parents. The isolation and freedom provide the opportunity for a teenage freshman entering college to transform into a young adult senior graduating college. It also provides a forum to test and enjoy more mature relationships.

The college experience not only provides you the opportunity to meet people who are like you; it gives you the opportunity to adopt and modify your beliefs and become a more rounded individual. This can expand the circle of people with whom you may have mutual understandings, and set the stage for starting a relationship that may lead to marriage.

Sometimes we recognize our compatibility with another person in an instant. We just 'click.' More often, it is a revelation and process that evolves more naturally over time. Sometimes, it's a combination of the two. What you have at the culmination of this discovery process (which never really ends) are two individuals who finish each other's sentences, reach for each other's hands at the same time without thinking, and share a voluminous archive of inside jokes that no one else in the world could ever understand. And trust me, it's wonderful.

If you meet your potential partner in college, I still suggest that you experience the 'real world' for a year or two after graduation before committing to marriage. Your mutual understandings need some day-in and day-out exercise, and some real-world exposure, before you sign up for The Big One.

'That's just the way we do things.' 'We'd never consider that.' These are statements that you'll hear married couples with strong, broad mutual understandings say. One spouse isn't speaking on behalf of the other who is silent or absent. They're speaking on behalf of their common, often identical, way of thinking. This mindset is not simply the result of living together for a certain amount of time and learning about each other. This perspective is the result of two people whose childhood, adolescent, and young adult experiences — and the resulting values and beliefs — are very much shared.

These understandings have carried through into their adult and married lives seamlessly. They are the 'tent poles' that will hold your relationship up and give it shape. If you don't both share them, commit to carry them forward in your marriage, and live them out daily, you leave yourself susceptible to conflict and resentment, simply because you haven't made the same assumptions and don't feel the same way about what can seem to be obvious things.

If your spouse wants to own their own business, are you both aware of how much work is involved? If you both have that understanding, or better yet that experience in seeing the amount of work your parents or siblings invested in a business or profession, you're much better prepared to go through the experience yourself.

How do you handle a financial windfall? Some cultures have the tradition of having a big party and sharing the proceeds with the extended family. Other cultures are more private and encourage the married couple to handle the money — and even share the news — in their own time and their own way.

Once again, you want to try to be 'on the same page' as your spouse with these mutual understandings. It can happen that two people from very different backgrounds can have plenty of beliefs in common, but, most often, our environments and experiences shape us to such an extent that we gravitate to someone who has shared these.

Most of the time, too, we are able to be comfortable and function well in the company of someone who has a clear, empathetic picture of our past. Of course, they need to embrace and support our vision of the future, too. The balance is to marry someone who 'gets where you're coming from', figuratively and literally, yet is different enough to compliment and complete you.

It can be tempting, charming, and oh-so-clever to date someone who is the polar opposite of you, who comes from the other side of the tracks, who's exotic and maybe even a little dangerous. You can appear open-minded and even *avant garde*. I encourage you to be open-minded, not just appear to be so, and beware of trying to appear *avant garde*, as most people can tell when you're trying.

If you were raised in an affluent, traditional household, meeting the 'bad boy' who sweeps you off your feet with his devil-may-care attitude can be a thrilling experience. I encourage you to have your thrills, within limits. However, when it comes time to seriously consider a partner for life, you probably want to hitch your wagon to someone who sees things the way you do and is going in the same direction.

Note: there is one mutual understanding that may trump all others. It is important that you and your spouse have a *commitment to growth*; a commitment to evolving and becoming better people; a commitment to examining any outdated ideas you have or share, and letting them go or revising them in light of new experiences or information.

This process is something that you share with your partner, even if you don't always do it with your partner. You continue to learn, grow, and change as an active and conscious choice. It makes you a better person. It also makes you a better partner. You and your spouse must be in agreement with this one big understanding, or one of you will grow and one of you won't, and someone will be left behind, regardless of how much you have in common at the start of your marriage.

Questions to Ask and Answer

- ♥ What are at least ten mutual understandings you and your partner share at present?

- ♥ How many childhood experiences do you share with your spouse? What were they?

- ♥ Are adolescent and young adult experiences you had in common? What were they?

- ♥ How similar are your beliefs about marriage and work to your parents' beliefs?

- ♥ How similar are your partner's beliefs about marriage and work to your parents' beliefs?

- ♥ How similar are your beliefs about marriage and work to your partner's parents' beliefs?

- ♥ Do you both have a commitment to growth?

- ♥ Does your spouse automatically know how they're supposed to dress for a particular social function?

- ♥ Do you have to advise them or ask them to put on nicer clothes?

Your Household

As the first place and space you share as a married couple, your household will function as your residence, the environment in which you spend the most time together, and your individual and joint sanctuary from the outside world. It will also be the place in which you entertain friends, family, and colleagues. It will reflect your sense of order, your values, your aspirations, and your tastes.

If at all possible, it is critical that you and your spouse enter a neutral space. By that I mean it is important that you move into a new place together. This new place is not a place that you have been living in for a period of time and that you call 'yours.' Nor is it a place where your partner has lived for a period of time and that he or she can call 'mine.'

You should move into a new place, unload and unpack boxes together, discuss the arrangement of the furniture and where you will hang pictures, and enjoy your first meal at your first kitchen table together. Many times this first meal is from a local Chinese food restaurant, delivered, which you eat out of the cartons with plastic forks and enjoy with a bottle of wine and a single lit candle. This happens because you haven't found the box that contains the silverware and plates, and after a day of unpacking, cooking is the last thing you want to do. Also, the utilities may not have been turned on yet.

Nevertheless, this may be the most romantic dinner of your life. It signals the start of your life together in your own place.

As you unpack, organize, and decorate your first residence, it should reflect both your personal styles and be functional for the life that you're going to lead together. Women who go overboard with the chintz and men who try to bring the man cave into the living room don't do their partners any favors. The common areas of the residence and the master bedroom need to be visually pleasant and workable on a daily basis for both partners.

In "The Old Money Book" I detail how you can furnish your place quite nicely without breaking the bank or wasting money on cheap furniture. Refer to the 'Furnishings' section of that book if you like. It will help you build a collection of sturdy, elegant, and functional furniture that will endure much of your married life.

If you have a spare bedroom that will be a common office, it has to be arranged to suit both of you. You're going to collect a volume of documents in your married life, and keeping them accessible and organized is going to be essential if you want to maintain your sanity when an insurance company or a doctor needs information. Consider a small, three-drawer filing cabinet to house your new family's documents. Create tabs and files that fit your needs. 'Taxes' will inevitably be one of these, I'm sorry to say. So will 'Medical', 'Lease Agreement' or 'Mortgage', 'Automobiles', 'Checking and Savings Accounts', 'Investments,' and 'Will' or 'Family Trust.'

Of course, you may want to keep originals of vital documents like birth certificates and marriage certificates in a fireproof lockbox or in a safe deposit box at your local bank. Whatever you choose to do, start and stay organized as you go through life together. It's one less factor contributing to stress between two people.

Another factor that you want to address and stay on top of is keeping your residence clean and orderly. It is best to sit down and have a heart-to-heart talk about how this is going to be achieved. If both partners are working at jobs forty hours a week, the cleaning of dirt and putting away of things should be shared equally between the two of you. You may also opt for a person to come and clean your residence. It is important that you keep your place looking and feeling nice. Physically, you will be sick less often because your place will harbor fewer germs and less dust. Emotionally, you will feel better each time you enter your home from a long day at work. So, as in all matters marital, reach an agreement and honor it.

A less obvious aspect of your residence is this: your place is the place where all of your personal, intimate business as a couple remains. You don't have an argument at home, then run off to tell Daddy what an awful toad your husband is. You may have made up with Mr. Wonderful the next day, but the tearful conversation you had with Daddy will remain in his mind as he sits across the dinner table from your spouse next Sunday. That's not fair.

You're going to make love with each other, fight with one another, and conspire against neighbors, relatives, and the world, all within the confines of your residence. Keep your personal affairs private and within those four walls. Present a unified and harmonious front to the world. It may seem hypocritical, and it is, but nobody wants to hear about your problems. Furthermore, it's not fair to share them with anyone other than a priest, a qualified therapist, or whatever name or image you give to your personal God.

You'll have a bitter disagreement. Still, you will be obligated to attend a social event. You will argue fiercely until the moment the hostess opens her front door and warmly welcomes you inside. You will then smile instantly and tell her how lovely it is to see her. You will go inside together and greet all the other married people at the party. We will probably be able to tell that you've been arguing. So we will offer to get you a drink, talk about the food the hostess is serving, or sports. We will not mention the fact that you look like hell warmed over. We know it will pass. We've all been there. An hour later, you and your spouse will have cooled down. You'll squeeze each other's hand as we all laugh about something that happened last week. And it will end up being a great evening.

You'll return to your residence, kick off your shoes, and embrace. Your disagreement is over. Now it's time to talk about how positively awful some of the party guests looked.

And that's fine. You can do that. You're at home.

Questions to Ask and Answer

- ♥ Between you and your partner, which of you is neater?
- ♥ Between you and your partner, which of you is more organized?
- ♥ Did either or both of you grow up with household chores that you were responsible for?
- ♥ Did either of both of you grow up with household staff who cleaned the house?
- ♥ Did either or both of you grow up sharing a room with siblings as a child?
- ♥ Did either or both of you have your own room as a child?
- ♥ Did either or both of you share a room in college?
- ♥ Does either or both of you know how to cook?
- ♥ Does either or both of you know how to do laundry?
- ♥ Does either or both of you know how to iron a shirt or blouse?
- ♥ Do you share the same standards of cleanliness with regards to your residence?
- ♥ How will you compensate for any differences in your standards?

Your Finances

It's common knowledge that financial stress is a leading cause of conflict in marriage and a huge contributor to divorce. You simply can't minimize the importance of money. Very few people can honestly say they care nothing about it. Most of those who can are either very rich or, like sadhus in India, have forsaken the material world in pursuit of spiritual enlightenment.

There is the obvious need for money in order to function on a daily basis: we buy and eat food; we pay rent or a mortgage for shelter; we buy and wear clothes. But the more crucial aspect of how money colors our lives is the emotional one. How do we feel about money? What does it mean to us? These are difficult questions for most people to answer. Not because they don't want to know the answers, but because sometimes it's a challenge to get to the root of the experiences or beliefs that shape our attitude toward money and result in how we handle it.

A common core emotion for most people when they think about money is the fear or insecurity they feel if for some reason they don't have enough of it. This concern drives many of us to get a good education, work, save, invest, and spend carefully throughout our lives. We don't want to be without money.

Conversely, there may also be the sense of security or positive self-esteem that many of us feel when we have a surplus or abundance of it. This feeling comes from knowing that we can handle an unexpected event or emergency. We have more options when it comes to where we're going to live. We can buy things we like. We can travel. We can spend, or we have the option to simply hold on to the money.

Many of the things we do that relate to money are the result of childhood experiences. If our parents didn't save a dime and spent everything they earned, we might have insecurity about money and be frugal. If our parents saved every dime but didn't really enjoy life, we might be extravagant as a way of expressing our resentment. If there's a huge financial change of circumstances during our childhood or adolescence—going from rags to riches or vice versa—who knows how that would make us feel or behave?

The emotional landscape we're covering here is as unique as every individual on the planet. Still, I'm going to provide you with some basic guidelines that will help you make money less of an issue in your marriage.

Note: money will always be an issue in your marriage. For very poor couples, the issue is having enough. For very rich couples, the issue is what to do with it. For those in the middle, congratulations: it's both of those.

This may be the most important information you take from this book because it is difficult to be happy with someone who doesn't have the same attitudes and beliefs about money as you do. You can barely go on a two week vacation with them, much less build a life with them. So let's get this right.

The first thing you need is a clear picture of your attitudes and beliefs about money. I would encourage you and your partner to sit down and write a financial history of your family and share it with each other. This will include what you heard happened in your family—'My grandfather invested in a small oil company, it went public, and he made a lot of money.' It will also include what you experienced first-hand — 'My father spent everything that he inherited.'

As you share this information, you'll need to also share how the particular event you're recounting *made you feel*. This is the most important thing you can identify and articulate. These feelings that you have shape your behavior toward money.

You will also share your childhood experiences about how you, personally, spent and saved money. Are you still spending and saving the same way now as an adult? Unless some seismic shift in your thinking has occurred, you probably are.

If you have chosen to marry someone who shares your social class and educational experience, you will probably have less terrain to navigate on this issue. However, there will always be some differences in philosophy between two people regarding money, no matter how in love or in sync they are with each other. You simply have to be honest, communicate, listen, compromise, agree, and move forward.

As a couple, you're going to have income — money coming in to your household from work or investments. The question for you as a couple now becomes, 'What do we do with it?' This question arises because you want to have enough to survive and prosper, as well as enjoy life and the fruits of your labor.

In even simpler terms, you can categorize you money as Income, Expenses, Saving/Investing, and Spending. Obviously, you've discussed how you as a couple and as individuals are going to have income. This may involve jobs, investments, or business ownership. Next, you're going to have expenses. This involves shelter, transportation, food, medical care, and clothing, among other things. Any positive difference between Income and Expenses leaves the amount for Saving/Investing and Spending.

If you're like most couples, you have a fairly good idea of what your Income is going to be and what your Expenses are going to be. You've probably made a budget for that. Where the ambiguity and the possibility for conflict arise is in the areas of Saving/Investing and Spending. This is where values, social class, and education experience come into play. This is where emotional surprises like stinginess and the desire for social status also get a chance to come out and dance around the kitchen table like characters from a bad fairy tale.

How you as a couple agree to handle money and the harmony with which you achieve that accord is very telling. Here's a short list of what it tells you:

- ♥ It tells you if you're going in the same direction in life.
- ♥ It tells you if you have the same values.
- ♥ It tells you if you have the same understanding of delayed gratification.
- ♥ It tells you if you have the same perspective on material possessions.
- ♥ It tells you if you have the same tolerance for risk.
- ♥ It tells you what your priorities are, as a couple and as individuals.

You simply can't underestimate the importance of the way you and your partner see and act with money.

You might be reading this and simply saying to yourself, 'Well, that's all fine and good, but my spouse is going to make all the financial decisions for us. He's very good at that, and I'm sure it will all be fine.' I have known several people who have made that choice, and the consequences for that lack of involvement have been disastrous for almost all of them.

I would encourage you and your partner to have a thousand disagreements about money before simply handing the reigns over to one partner in a marriage. I would also caution you strongly about having a third party manage your money unless your income and assets are very substantial and the demands on both your schedules are just as substantial. At that point, there are business management firms who act as a 'family office' for high net worth families and individuals. If you're not in that position, sit down at the kitchen table once or twice a month and have a ten-minute conversation about your finances so both of you are informed and involved. I know billionaires and their spouses who do this, so don't think you're above it or too good for it.

I am not saying that you and your partner must be completely in agreement about all your financial decisions. That's not realistic. You simply have to reach agreements about major things and move forward. When conflicts come up about smaller things, you discuss them. As with all things in marriage, you have to really assess how important this issues is to you or your spouse and why. Only then can you take steps to reach a mutually satisfactory, and even fulfilling, solution.

Some couples have agreements in which they automatically save a certain percentage of their total household income. Not surprisingly, the higher that percentage, the sooner the couple is financially independent. Some couples commit one partner's earnings completely to savings and live on the other partner's earnings. Not surprisingly, the couple who does this will be financially independent sooner than a couple who spends most of both incomes and saves only sporadically.

Credit card debt is a huge problem for many couples. I think it is easily the biggest financial danger couples face. You can handle illness, unemployment, and other emergencies so much more easily if you don't have credit card debt. If you don't have it, don't get it. If you have it, get rid of it. If you can't control your spending, cut up your credit cards and get professional help. *Eliminating and avoiding credit card debt should be the top financial priority in your marriage.*

One thing I should mention at this point is the purchasing of gifts for each other now that you're married. In all likelihood, 'my money' and 'your money' will cease to exist when you get married. It will be 'our' money. So if you go out and buy a new car for your partner, put a big red bow on it and park it in the driveway as a surprise, don't deceive yourself: you've spent your money — and your partner's — on that gift. If it's not in the budget you've both agreed upon and are working to honor, it might not be a pleasant surprise.

My advice is to set a limit on the amount of money that you will spend on each other for holidays, anniversaries, and birthdays. You'll find that in spending less you have to think more. You'll come up with gifts that are more meaningful, more thoughtful, and much more fun.

All of the things I've discussed so far may seem fairly obvious. You would think that most couples have a handle on their finances, communicate about them regularly and productively, and are setting aside a predictable and substantial portion of their income for Savings/Investing. If you look at the financial statistics for most American households, they don't and they aren't.

Why? Because many times there is a gap between what people intellectually know they should do and what they actually do on a daily basis. The more you reduce this gap, the better you live.

Obstacles that increase or maintain this gap include habit and exposure to influence. If you have the habit of spending money on things you don't need in order to feel better about yourself, you probably know that the behavior isn't beneficial. But habits can be hard to break. So you determine why you're doing it, who you're hurting by doing it, and what factors are contributing to it. I think the biggest thing you can do, and always the first step, is simply to identify a bad habit. When you've done that and realize you're hurting yourself and others, you're halfway to a solution.

One of the major factors contributing to unhealthy behavior, like spending or eating fast food, is exposure to influence, most often advertising. Business owners spend billions of dollars on advertising not because they think it's entertaining or fun, but because it works. It affects our decision-making process. It creates familiarity with their products. It creates a desire and can even create what we think is a need. You want to limit yourself to exposure to advertising on television, in magazines, and online. You want to give yourself, your partner, and your new family every opportunity in life. Being financially healthy is a big part of that.

Two things that couples don't usually address as they start life together are *windfall* and *opportunity*. By windfall, I mean the infusion of an unexpected and substantial amount of money, real estate, or other asset into your household. Most often, this is an inheritance.

For a couple who have been holding down two jobs, paying the bills, and trying to save for years or even decades, the sudden influx of cash or something very much like it can be a wonderful event. It can also be challenging. The wonderful part of it is easy to understand. Most often, it provides a momentary or permanent break from financial worry. It can provide a sense of security for a couple. They can pay off debt or purchase a necessity. They can take a deep breath.

With a little thought, the challenging part can be easy to imagine, too. Depending upon the size and nature of the windfall, one or both partners can go off the rails with spending and celebration. Circumstances become ripe for substance abuse and infidelity. Couples can disagree on how to save, spend, or invest the windfall. It can all go very wrong very easily. The saddest thing is when someone sees, for the first time, an unpleasant aspect of their partner revealed through what they initially thought was a blessing.

If you or your partner are an OMG (an Old Money Guy or Old Money Gal), you may have already received an inheritance. That experience, coupled with the Core Values you may have been raised with, may have equipped you with the tools to handle a windfall properly. If you are unfamiliar with this type of event, I can only offer this advice: immediately consult a certified public accountant about the tax implications for you and your partner; go out to dinner and celebrate with the money you have in your pocket; and wait six months before you touch the money from the windfall.

During this six month cooling-off period, you and your partner will have at least a dozen great ideas of how to spend or invest your newfound fortune. Honestly, they're probably all terrible. That's why I'm giving you six months: to let you run all your bad ideas around the block a few times before you see what stinking, mangy, flea-bitten dogs they really are.

Let me throw some rocks at the most common canines:

- ♥ New Car: You probably don't need a new car. You might *want* a new car, but you probably don't require one to continue to function. How do I know this? Because if you really needed one you would have already bought one prior to the windfall.

- ♥ New Home: You may *want* to move into a new residence, perhaps a new home. With your new windfall, you can make a down payment easily. What you may not be able to do as easily is pay the property taxes and cover the increased maintenance costs on that new McMansion.

- ♥ New Jewelry: You may think you or your spouse *deserves* a new piece of jewelry or a watch. The truth is you simply want it. What you and your partner truly deserve is an intelligent, circumspect, and mature decision-making process that maximizes this windfall for the long-term benefit of your family.

In short, you and your partner would be best served to digest and adjust to any financial windfall very slowly, very privately, and with the advice and direction of tax professionals who regularly counsel clients who have a net worth equal to or greater than yours. All of your family, some of your friends, and a few of your coworkers will have ideas for investments or investment advisors. Observe the six-month rule. Talk it over at length. Feel free to have conflicting emotions and feel free to change your mind about how you feel about anything relating to this windfall.

What a financial windfall does for a couple is that it provides them an *opportunity*. Managed properly, a financial windfall can pay for a child's education, provide for the acquisition of income-producing assets, or simply enhance a couple's financial nest egg.

It can also provide the resources for one or both partners to take a risk. It may provide the capital for the couple to start or invest in a business or pursue a career that does not have a consistent, reliable income. (For some reason, writing comes to mind.) When considering taking a risk with the proceeds from a windfall, it is absolutely essential that much research and much communication occur. It is also critical that both partners be completely on board and aware of the factors and the risks involved in the decision.

You always want to hope for the best, but if you can't live with the worst, you may not want to commit to a particular risk. If great things come from the risk, know and acknowledge that you have done it together. If it fails, know that you both made the decision with your eyes wide open. Look for lessons you can learn from the failure, and then move on without regrets or resentment.

Set financial goals together. Work toward them together. Review them frequently. Communicate. Adjust. Celebrate. Thrive.

Questions to Ask and Answer

- Were your parents considered rich, poor, or middle class?
- Did they talk to you about money?
- What did they say?
- How did you feel about money as a child?
- Did you have an allowance?
- Did you have required household chores?
- Did you save money as a child?
- Did you have summer jobs?
- Did you have part-time jobs in college?
- Did you pay your own college tuition?
- In college, were you on a budget or could you spend whatever amount you wanted?
- What are your financial goals for this year and five years from now?
- What are you doing on a daily basis to accomplish those?
- Who do you discuss money and financial issues with?
- Do your friends know how much money you have?
- What do you think you would do with a financial windfall of $10,000?
- What do you think you would do with a financial windfall of $100,000?
- What do you think you would do with a financial windfall of $1,000,000?
- Have you received an inheritance in the past?

- ♥ What did you do with it?
- ♥ Do you shop for clothing or consumer products (non-food items) on a weekly basis?
- ♥ Do you shop for clothing or consumer products (non-food items) on a monthly basis?
- ♥ Do you shop for clothing or consumer products only when you really need them?
- ♥ What do you think money can do for you and your partner?

Your Health

Your overall physical well-being is contingent upon diet, exercise, hygiene, your mental state, and a little heredity. Four out of the five of those are within your control. The easiest way to control your health is through habits. You either have good ones or bad ones. You either exercise regularly or you don't. Both choices become habits.

Habits that influence your health may be the most important ones you will adopt during your lifetime. The state of your physical well-being will color every area of your life. You probably already know this. What you may now want to consider is that you're going to be married and share your life with another person. Your habits don't just shape your world; they directly impact the quality of life of the person you marry.

Conversely, the health habits of the person you marry will directly impact the quality of your life. If either one of you or both of you eats junk food, adopts a sedentary lifestyle, drinks to excess, or smokes cigarettes, don't be surprised if, over the course of your life together, you're not feeling well, sick, in the hospital, on prescription medication, undergoing surgery, and dying a premature and painful death. And finally, when these things happen, please don't wonder why it happened. It's not the work of some mean and heartless God. It's the things you did to your body.

If you haven't guessed by now, I'm going to communicate some hard truths in this section. I'm going to say some things that may seem harsh and dogmatic. What I'm actually doing is saving you and your partner a lot of pain in the future, if you heed my advice. The reason I'm sharing this information in such a brutal fashion is because I have experienced illness within a marriage. Luckily, everything turned out well.

It turned out well partly because my wife and I lead very healthy lives. We exercise daily, eat fresh foods, don't smoke cigarettes, and drink only occasionally. We see the dentist regularly. We get regular check-ups. We try to moderate the stress in our lives. We enjoy a good laugh. We meditate and do yoga. We have a spiritual philosophy.

It is my most sincere hope that you and your partner have a marriage in which both of you are healthy the entire time you're together. There is a chance, however, that a serious illness may present itself during your married life. The thing you want to do is live a healthy life so that if you do get sick, it's an illness that is not the result of bad habits or negligence on your part. You also want to be healthy so that your recovery time is shorter. You want to be healthy because there's no suffering like seeing your spouse suffer. It really motivates you to get well quickly and never get sick again.

If you have to be in the hospital, you want it to be from breaking a leg on the ski slopes trying to go too fast, not losing a lung from cigarette smoking for the past twenty years.

Note: If you are considering marrying someone who has a disability or a serious family history of a disease, you must, in all fairness, ask yourself some tough questions about how your life together will be on a daily basis. Can you handle the responsibilities of being a caretaker? What sacrifices will you make to share a life with this person? Is it worth it to you? You have to also consider probable outcomes. Does this disease affect life expectancy? How do children figure into the equation? What are their chances of being healthy? I'm not being mean. I'm not being cruel. I'm not saying that that marriage is only for physically perfect people. I'm encouraging you to be honest with yourself and your partner about everything, prior to making a commitment, by looking at life on a daily basis, as well as a decade or two down the road.

Now we come to the harsh(er) part, specifically about cigarette smoking.

If you're dating and playing the field, I'm going to suggest that you not go on one date with a person who smokes cigarettes. If you follow this advice, it is highly unlikely that you will ever marry a person who smokes cigarettes.

You will not have to be around when they are diagnosed with emphysema, lung cancer, or a veritable buffet of other illnesses which will truncate their life expectancy and eventually kill them. You will also be less susceptible to sickness and disease due to exposure to second-hand smoke. Your children will be less likely to have respiratory infections, too.

If you are presently in a relationship with someone who smokes cigarettes, I would urge you to communicate your concerns about your partner's health. If you are not married to this person, and they are unwilling to stop smoking, I encourage you to break off the relationship. You need to find someone who cares more about their health, and more about yours.

If you are married to someone who smokes cigarettes, I would encourage you to be as vocal, persistent, and supportive as humanly possible to get them to quit. There are an abundance of resources at your disposal. Use them.

Surprisingly, as bad as cigarettes are for your health, they aren't as bad as living a sedentary lifestyle. By that I mean…sitting at a desk all day at work, then riding home in a car or on the subway, then sitting at a table for dinner, then sitting and watching television or tapping on the laptop.

You and your potential spouse must commit to one another and support one another in living an active lifestyle. Don't tell me you don't have time. Unless you're a guest of the government in a correctional facility not of your choosing, you do what you want to do.

Don't go on a diet. Eat fresh foods and avoid processed foods. Buy a stationary bike and use it. Go for a walk, take the stairs. Have three days a week in which you read a book and don't watch television. Meditate. Do yoga.

Questions to Ask and Answer

There aren't any.
You know what to do. Do it.

Your Social Circle

One of the most important sources of joy and support during your marriage will come from your social circle of family, friends, and colleagues. You want to make every effort to maintain, nurture, and grow relationships that belong to you, your partner, and both of you.

You may enter into your marriage with a shared group of friends. You and your spouse may have respective friendships that you've maintained from college. Your families may live nearby. Professional relationships may have blossomed into friendships over time.

Whatever the topography of your social circle, it's important to keep these relationships strong. The danger is that, during the courtship and honeymoon phases of your relationship, you may feel that your beloved is the center of the universe and that you need no one else in your life. Of course, that's not the case. Most of us pull out of that once our relationship develops and matures.

There are several reasons you want to have a circle of friends and family around you and your spouse. First, it's an opportunity to laugh and share. Not to be a snob (I know, you're saying 'Too late!'), but your friends should be generally upbeat and optimistic people. After spending an afternoon or evening with them, you should feel better, not worse. Yes, everyone has problems and challenges in life. Yes, you want to be there for people you care about. However, knowing when and how to share those troubles is important, for you and your friends. If someone can't come to a party and enjoy themselves, it makes a relationship difficult. A healthy social circle gives you a chance to let off some steam, catch up with others, celebrate life, and set your worries aside for a moment.

Second, when you socialize you realize that other married people have problems, too. You shouldn't take particular pleasure in this (okay, maybe a little here and there), but it will help you maintain perspective when you want to strangle your spouse for not putting the cap back on the toothpaste. You'll visit with other husbands and wives and, while not talking out of school or betraying your own spouse's trust, you will be able to communicate a shared understanding about the joys and challenges of being married.

Third, having a circle of friends that you do things with will allow you to return home to your spouse with something interesting to talk about. The time away will make your time together more vibrant. Your hobbies and outside interests were probably part of the reason your spouse found you so attractive — or even irresistible — in the first place. Don't stop doing them. That said, if your spouse isn't keen on a dangerous or life-threatening activity that you enjoy, you have to give it up and find something else. That's just the way it is.

Fourth, socializing with people gives you the opportunity to become a full-blown hypocrite. You'll shake hands and make small talk with people you don't like, and you may even start to like them, which is shocking but somehow inspiring. As I've mentioned, you'll get to act happy immediately after having had an argument with your spouse just prior to a social event. Just as surprisingly, acting happy will start to make you happy. You may resent this, but that, too, is part of it.

You'll learn to feign interest when people tell you about their hip replacement. You'll learn, too, that the phrase, 'How are you?' is more often a standard greeting than a sincere inquiry. You'll learn to say, 'I'm well, thank you,' even if you're not. Others will appreciate this because, to a certain extent, we're all suffering through the socializing until we run into someone who we can really talk to. This is the way the world works. Welcome to it.

Fifth, you will need to socialize in order to move you and your spouse's career forward. Much of what I mentioned in the previous paragraph applies to that kind of socializing. Remember to be polite to everyone, make friends with the boss's wife, and don't drink too much.

Sixth, you need to recognize your spouse's accomplishments and special days in a social setting. Your spouse will put up with a lot from you all year long. Throw a birthday party to show you appreciate it. Have the family over for an anniversary dinner. Acknowledge the support they've provided your marriage. You don't have to spend a lot of money. You do have to make an effort.

Finally, you want to socialize because it gives you a chance to dress up, go out, slow dance, and roll the odometer back to your courtship days. You need these moments throughout your marriage to rekindle the spark. You need to remember why you fell in love with this person. You need to put your arms around your spouse and hold them tight, whether it's at a backyard barbeque or the Met gala. Sometimes it helps if you're away from your home, in the middle of a crowd, out of your routine. That separation from the familiar contributes to a reigniting of the intimate.

Embrace it and enjoy it.

Questions to Ask and Answer

- ♥ When is your anniversary?
- ♥ When is your spouse's birthday?
- ♥ What have you planned for those two days?

Your Work

The work that you and your spouse do throughout your married life is going to shape the nature of your lives together to a large extent. It will certainly determine the income level you have, how much time you spend at work, whether or not you have to travel frequently or relocate occasionally, and may even determine where you live permanently and the people you associate with. The nature of your work will determine your schedule, your social life, whether or not you have to bring work home with you, and how much time you get to spend with your spouse.

As we've discussed, almost all careers have a social element to them. You will be expected to attend business social functions that relate to your spouse's work, and they will be expected to do the same for you. More importantly, some industries have a 'culture,' corporate or otherwise, that members of that industry are expected to understand, adapt to, and participate in.

If you and your spouse both work, professional demands may influence when (and if) you have children and how you raise them. Will they be in the care of a nanny, day care facility, or member of your extended family? Will you be able to take maternity or paternity leave? Who will be the primary caregiver during the first few months and years of a child's life? A more pointed question is who will put their career on hold if a child is born and for how long?

If you are or plan to be self-employed, the considerations and planning required for married life are even more involved. You must consider the possibility of fluctuating income, the financial investment in your business or profession, as well as medical and life insurance for your spouse and family in case something happens to you.

An equally important consideration is what impact the typical long hours and rare vacations are going to have on your spouse and how you're going to address those fairly and effectively. Making a lot of money helps, but it is not a cure for all ills. Let me say that again: Making a lot of money helps, but it is not a cure for all ills.

Human beings require emotional support, not just financial support. You must acknowledge the emotional needs of your spouse as you plan to get married and pursue an entrepreneurial endeavor or creative career. A spouse will stay with you longer and you will be happier together longer if you provide them the emotional support they need over the course of the marriage. If you make a lot of money, but are not physically and/or mentally present to provide your spouse emotional support, the money alone will not keep the marriage alive. Not a real marriage, anyway.

It's important to recognize and acknowledge the impact that living in a digital age has on our work and our relationships. Thanks to the internet and mobile devices, we can be, and often are, in constant communication with the outside world. Our colleagues expect us to be available immediately and almost constantly. The idea of turning off or leaving your cell phone behind when you go on vacation is unfathomable to most people.

Much of this mindset, for working adults, is propagated by the workplace environment and the media. Some of it is, admittedly, simply the speed at which business is done in today's world. Some of it is a myopic sense of our own self-importance that exists only in our mind. An atmosphere dominated by technology poses a real and present danger to human relationships, especially a marriage.

The omnipresent, pervasive intrusion of an electronic device into every aspect of our lives is not healthy. It's detrimental to our communication skills, ironically enough. We can't form grammatically correct sentences, but we can damn sure text like a bat out of hell. We can have millions of search results for billions of topics, but we can't focus long enough to read, digest, and make considered applications of the knowledge we have at our fingertips.

And forget having a conversation with someone who is constantly on their phone. Much of this intrusion, this infection of the human experience, is social. How essential social media is to your actual social life is something you're going to have to determine for yourself. I will tell you this: you should make sure that you spend about the same amount of time online as your spouse, or else you're in for a bumpy ride. Why? Because it gets irritating and boring very quickly when you want to have a conversation or go for a walk and your spouse is engrossed in a silly cat video. It also makes for some dry conversation when you've read an interesting book and want to discuss it and your spouse recounts how funny the silly cat video was.

I will tell you this: you should individually and as a couple determine how, when, and under what circumstances you're going to go radio silent and shut down the electronic devices. This can be for a candlelit dinner, a long weekend away, or simply when you meditate or pray. This is part of compartmentalizing your work as it relates to your life. It is critical for your marriage that you have boundaries for your work.

If you always take a business call at any hour of the day or night, you run the risk of making your spouse feel like they are not a priority. Of course, many times when the phone rings, they're going to say, 'Oh, go ahead, honey, take the call.' That's what spouses are supposed to say when a coworker calls you during dinner. What they really want to do is throw your phone against the wall.

Commit to your work. Acknowledge its demands. Establish boundaries. If you see these boundaries being crossed for a period of time or even an instant, communicate with your spouse. Apologize. Compensate for the intrusion with something that will please your spouse. Don't let it happen again.

Questions to Ask and Answer

- What profession or job will you have when you're married?
- What profession or job will your spouse have when you're married?
- What are the demands of your profession or job? (Make a list.)
- What are the demands of your spouse's profession or job? (Make another list.)
- Over the course of a seven day week, what do you expect the daily calendar and schedule to look like for you and your spouse?
- Will you have weekends off?
- Will you be required to bring work home?
- What is the possibility of overtime?
- What is the possibility of promotion?
- What does that involve?
- Does your work require you or your spouse to travel?
- Will you or your spouse continue your education in order to enhance your employment opportunities? (Advanced college degrees or specialized training)
- How will this impact your schedule and household budget?
- How could this enhance your household income?
- Do you or your spouse plan to start or buy a business?
- What financial and time demands will this endeavor require?
- When or if you decide to have children, who will be the primary caregiver for the first five years of the child's life?

- ♥ Who will put their career on hold in order to have and raise a child?
- ♥ Is your work a large part of your identity?
- ♥ Is your work simply a job that you do?

Your In-Laws And Extended Family

One of the big contradictions in marriage is that, on the one hand, on the day of your wedding, you usually unite two families. You invite them to now become a larger family based on your union. On the other hand, you and your spouse establish a new, independent entity as a married couple. You displace your parents, siblings, and extended family and make each other your new priority.

Parents, as well-intentioned and hopeful as they are, will have difficulty with this most of the time. They have given birth to you. They have raised you. They may think they know you better than anyone in the world, and they may be right. However, they must accept that you've made a considered, deliberate, and intelligent choice. There is behavior that comes with this acceptance: it's called minding your own business.

As your parents and in-laws go through the process of accepting this new relationship with you and your spouse, you will have to go through the process of being not only an adult, but a married adult. There's a big difference. An adult might share everything with her mother, just as she's done since she was a child. A married adult doesn't. An adult might run home to Daddy every time her feelings get hurt. A married adult doesn't. An adult might ask Dad for a quick loan if there's a *cash flow problem*. A married adult doesn't.

Your parents probably bought you things as a child, and even as an adult. They obviously did this because you needed things — food and clothing come to mind — but there may be other motivations for buying you things. They may have wanted to elicit certain behavior from you, so they bought you something you wanted. I'd be too harsh to call this a bribe, but it might be called positive reinforcement in some psychology circles. They may have withheld money or material things in order to punish you. They may have felt they neglected you in some way and tried to compensate by buying you things.

You may want to analyze some of your parents' behavior in the past if it continues and seems to be a problem when you get married. Ironically, your spouse may be able to see this behavior for what it is much more clearly than you can. They are new to it and distanced from it because they haven't grown up with it.

Your parents may simply be happy for you and want to be generous. However, as a newly married couple, you need to establish yourself and your independence. Accept appropriate wedding and house-warming gifts if you can honestly say there are no strings attached. If you and your spouse don't feel comfortable accepting something, simply decline and say, "You know, we really appreciate the offer, but that's something we'd like to do (or buy) for ourselves," or something polite along those lines. If either one of you isn't comfortable with a gift, don't accept it. There may be hurt feelings in the short run, but, if you articulate your position politely but firmly, there will be more respect for you as a married couple in the long run.

Most parents will understand a couple's desire to work, earn money, and purchase things together, on their own. It gives a sense of fulfillment and accomplishment that you don't get from someone giving something to you. Usually, when you express your desire to do or acquire something on your own, it will be respected and admired.

If it isn't, this is a great opportunity to do something that you will, as a married couple, probably do several times during the course of your marriage with issues great and small: tell the rest of the world to go to hell.

You may not actually say it to someone, and I suggest that you rarely do, but you will have to disregard the agendas of others on a fairly regular basis.

Other people, even those you love, will sometimes be unhappy with your choices, especially when they want to give you something that you don't want or feel it's best not to accept. You and your spouse will make your choices and live with them. You and your spouse can be happy with those choices, and, like I said, everybody else can go to hell.

Conversely, you may have been self-reliant or even prosperous as an adolescent and young adult. Your parents (or siblings) may have come to you for money, expecting that you'd always give it because, 'Hey, we're family.' If this is the case, you're going to have to set up some definitive boundaries now that you're married. It does not matter how much money you have or how little your family asks for; it's the fact that once you are married, they are not asking you for money. They are asking you and your spouse for money. Once again, there's a big difference.

Loaning or giving money to members of your extended family will be a critical issue to address in order to preserve harmony in your marriage and achieve your financial goals. Every time you consider loaning money, you risk losing both the money and the relationship. That's enough of a risk with a friend. That's a huge risk with a family member. It's going to be enough of a learning curve for you and your partner to find your footing in managing your financial affairs together. The last thing you need is a member of your extended family coming to you for money.

I do realize that things happen. There are emergencies. However, you should really consider the mindset of a person who approaches newlyweds for a loan, family member or not. *It's not cricket.*

Another bit of tricky business you'll encounter with your extended family is how much of your success you're going to show or share, if any, and how you'll do that. I will tell you this: for every new car, fur coat, or new piece of jewelry you display to relatives who have less than you, you create, even in the most non-materialistic of people, an expectation that you'll share your success with them in some way at some point. You may also foster resentment and create distance in your relationships.

Those relatives with more money than you and your spouse probably won't care. They'll be happy for you, and maybe for themselves: they may be relieved that you're doing well and won't be asking them for money. (Wink, nod.)

I'm not saying that you should adjust all of your behavior based on what someone else might think. I am saying that you should be aware of how you come across to those closest to you, those who raised you and grew up with you, those who have been there for you.

If, over the course of your marriage, you do well in your profession, your extended family will probably know. The best way to handle it is to be generous in ways that do not involve material things. You can bring or cook all of the food at the next family gathering. You can rent a vacation home for two weeks and invite the family to come, visit, and enjoy for one of those weeks. Invite them to share in your success by including them.

Do not show off. Do not cop an attitude. When it's time to do the dishes, get in there with the rest of the girls and roll your sleeves up, even if you've made a million bucks in real estate. If you just hit it big with your company's IPO, you still sit on the same sofa with your in-laws on game day and watch it on TV. This is how you earn and maintain their respect, even if you already have their love.

Within the confines of your marriage, you will have disagreements. You will have heated arguments. Tears will be shed, and voices may be raised. However, you will not threaten, grab, push, slap, throw things at, or intimidate your spouse at any time. Nor will you be allowed to have any of these things done to you, regardless of your behavior or your spouse's behavior.

If you feel like you're getting ready to cross one of these lines, walk out of the room or walk out of the house. Tell your spouse, 'I'm sorry. I'm about to lose my temper. I have to leave.' And leave. Go somewhere else and cool down. When you've cooled down, return and try to approach the issue you're upset about in a calm(er)(ish) way.

Cross one of those lines and your marriage could be over. You could also find yourself in jail, unemployed, and a social pariah. Everybody knows this. I feel it's important to repeat it.

Now let me say this: in your marriage you're going to have unbelievably painful arguments, discussions, disagreements, differences of opinion, hurt feelings, emotional outbursts, and every other kind of unpleasant human interaction heretofore known or not yet devised by man. Call them whatever you want to call them. You'll want to scream and you probably will scream. So will your spouse.

What you will not do is call or run to your parents or extended family and talk about what an idiot your spouse is any time after one of the above-mentioned disagreements. Unless you have been the victim of domestic violence, you will keep your mouth shut. Why? Because two hours from now you'll realize that you were just acting out, or your spouse will apologize, or you'll both say you're sorry, you'll hug — and maybe more — you'll make up, and all will be right with your world.

But your family has just heard — and cannot as easily forget — that you were very upset and said your spouse was an idiot. You will have divulged private and very personal information about your marriage that nobody wants to know in the first place. In the second place, that's not fair to your spouse, especially when they have to sit down next Sunday for dinner with the same relatives. I've said this before. I'm saying it again.

Yes, your spouse will drive you crazy. How and when you share that news flash — which is not news to anyone else you tell who has ever been married — is something you need to be very careful about. This is especially true if that information gets back to your spouse and hurts them. They could feel betrayed that you shared what they rightly thought should have been a private disagreement.

Vent your frustrations to other married friends calmly, lightly, with humor and perspectives, if you must. Know what's personal and what is common. Someone feeling insecure about their looks is personal. Someone not putting the toilet seat down is common. Share details about your marriage sparingly. Criticize your mate in public at your peril.

Questions to Ask and Answer

- Did your parents indulge you with material possessions or money as a child?

- Did they continue to give you money after you were an adult?

- Were there expectations that accompanied this money?

- Do you have siblings who come to you for money?

- Do you have siblings who act like you are their second or substitute parent?

- Have you and your spouse discussed how you're going to handle requests for money from extended family members?

- Have you loaned money to a family member without telling your spouse?

- Have you borrowed or accepted money from a family member without telling your spouse?

- Do you have more, less, or about the same amount of money as members of your extended family?

- Do you contribute pretty much equally in effort and expense at family gatherings?

- Are you aware right now of one family member who constantly needs money?

- Have you discussed with your spouse how you might help him or her without loaning or giving money?

Your Personal Growth

If you're like most people, you're going to marry someone with whom you have a number of things in common. At the time of your wedding, you're going to feel like you're generally in the same place and starting off together in life pretty much on equal terms.

The differences you have will probably be viewed by yourself and others as ones that are complimentary to you and your partner. You may be more spontaneous, for example. Your partner may be more deliberate in their approach to things. These differences may cause some conflict, but overall, they will provide balance in the relationship.

Over time, you'll face what I'll call external challenges to your relationship — issues with family or career — that you'll face together and, as a result of these, you'll grow as individuals and as a couple.

You may face an internal challenge as a couple which will be the result of this: one of you is growing personally at a much faster rate than the other. By personal growth, I mean one of you is, for example, continuing their education for career enhancement or simply for pleasure, learning a new language, picking up new hobbies, constantly meeting new people, or reading new books for self-improvement or intellectual stimulation.

And one of you is not doing those things. Emotional distance can develop slowly and permanently in this situation if both partners don't both share a commitment to personal growth. Or, if both partners have no interest in improving themselves, then they'll probably be fine together, too, but, really, is that what you want?

You are probably wise to assess early on if your potential spouse has a natural interest in trying new things, travel, reading, and generally improving themselves mentally and physically. Once you marry, it may be tempting to get into a routine and become a little lazy about self-improvement. At this point, you may recognize that your partner is becoming a little sedentary or not engaging in activities that expand or challenge them on a regular basis. Or they may see it in you.

This is the time for encouragement, not criticism. You can suggest dance lessons or training for a 10K run; it really doesn't matter. What matters is that this conversation, like many you'll have in a marriage, should come from a place of love. Tell your partner that you've noticed they're not as active or enthusiastic about things as they normally are. Ask if something is wrong. Have some ideas about things you can do together, or things your partner might consider doing individually. You're not delivering good news. Be diplomatic. Consider when and where you will bring this up.

Most of the time, just providing someone the awareness that they've gotten into a slump is enough to pop them out of it. They'll pick up a new exercise routine, get back with the golf game, take that computer class, whatever it is that gets the blood flowing and keeps the brain cells going. When they do this, remember to compliment them sincerely when you see them in a better frame of mind or better shape.

There will be activities you do for personal growth that you do alone and that you do as a couple. You may have a gym membership to keep in shape. You may have a reading list to constantly expand your world view. You may do charity work to remind you of how good you really do have it.

Whatever you choose to do in this area of self-improvement should make you feel better after you do it. Sure, exercise may leave your muscles sore for a minute and trying to learn a new language may make you think blood is pouring out of your forehead as you try to find a word. However, overall, these activities should energize you and stimulate your thinking.

This is vitally important because at the end of each day, or certainly on the weekend, you're going to sit with your partner and have an extended conversation. Of course, you'll discuss the household, career, or family issues that are currently at the forefront. You will, however, want to bring more to the table. You do that by having spent a portion of your time learning something new. You've been at a cooking class or read a new book or started a new hobby or met a new person. Outside of work, what are you really passionate about? What do you find fascinating? Bring that to your marriage.

When your partner discusses his personal interests, ask questions. Learn a little bit about them. You'll find you bring out the best in each other when you support each other's passions and hobbies.

Someone once said that marriage is one long conversation. In some respects, that's true. Just how interesting that conversation is on a regular basis is up to you and your partner's commitment to personal growth.

Part of personal growth for you in your marriage may involve alcohol or drugs. You and your partner probably socialized together during your dating process. You probably know what each other's attitudes are towards alcohol and drugs, and, to some extent, you've accepted those attitudes and their subsequent habits even if you're not fully supportive.

You're certainly aware of the legal consequences and health risks that accompany drug use and alcohol abuse. You're certainly familiar with what an arrest and conviction for drinking and driving can do for your career, your wallet, your life, or someone else's life. You know the risks of possessing illegal substances or being around people who possess or distribute those substances. Now that you're married or about to be married, let it be me who reminds you that you're now *risking for two* when you choose to use drugs, abuse alcohol, or use poor judgment.

Marriages can survive and even thrive in an environment in which one spouse drinks regularly and one spouse doesn't. Marriages can be fine with both spouses partying hard on occasion. Marriages are not fine when one or both partners are drunk on a regular basis. They rarely do well in environments where drugs are used on a regular basis.

'I can handle it.' The last great proclamation of many men right before they wreck their car, wreck their marriages, overdose, or end up in jail. Drugs and alcohol are fine and dandy when life is fine and dandy. It's just one big party and everybody's having a great time.

It's when you just took a hit on the stock market or you've lost an important client or you've lost a family member and you need to paste over that pain or bounce right back. You're certain that Dr. Jack Daniels will have the right diagnosis. You're certain that a snort of coke will get you back in the game. Old saying: cocaine *will* make you a new man. And the first thing a new man needs is some more cocaine.

Suddenly, the party's over and you're hung over, sick, and still in pain. The problems you were trying to escape are still there, but now, you've got less money in the bank because you spent it on drugs. Or you've got no money in the bank because you had no idea your spouse's drug habit was that bad.

By now, you get my point. If you never use drugs, you'll never have a drug problem. If you never drink when you're driving, you will never be arrested for drinking and driving.

If you keep your alcohol intake between the lines, and *cut it out completely* when you're having trouble in your career, marriage, or life in general, you'll probably be fine. Get through the rough spots with a clear head. Enjoy a drink to relax or celebrate, if that's what you like to do.

If you get drunk and say or do something that hurts your spouse, you're just as responsible for your actions as if you did them when you were sober. That's the rule. Deal with it.

Finally, I may not be able to persuade you to moderate your substance abuse, but, at some point in time, your body will. There will come a time when you will not be able to party like a rock star and then hit the ground running at dawn the next morning. There may come a time when your doctor tells you your liver is shot from drinking too much. There may come a time when you can't remember what it was that you were going to say. The brain cells just won't fire anymore. You may come home one day to an empty house. Your spouse may have had enough and you were just too drunk or high to heed the warning signs.

So you can hear me now or hear me later. It's better to walk on the sidewalk than in the middle of the street, even if you're sure there's no traffic. You're married now. You're not walking alone.

Questions to Ask and Answer

- ♥ What do you do with your time outside work or school?
- ♥ What does your partner do with his/her time outside work or school?
- ♥ Do you and your partner exercise together or separately?
- ♥ Do you read books?
- ♥ Do you have a particular subject that interests you?
- ♥ If you work, are you taking continuing education classes?
- ♥ Do you speak a second language?
- ♥ Do you constantly increase your knowledge about your religion?
- ♥ Do you feel like you are constantly growing spiritually through prayer, mediation, reading, or ritual?
- ♥ Do you feel you are a better person today than you were last week? Last month? Last year?
- ♥ Do feel like you sometimes drink too much?
- ♥ Do you drink alone?
- ♥ Do you drink when things aren't going well?
- ♥ Do you use drugs?
- ♥ Can you quit drinking or doing drugs for a month and be fine? (Try it and see.)
- ♥ Does your family have a history of alcohol or drug abuse?

Children

Having children is one of the richest blessings and biggest challenges any married couple will face. There are hundreds if not thousands of books and online resources about how to raise them well. I suggest you make use of all of them. You may read all of them, understand every word, and believe that you are ready for parenthood. You are not.

Still, you must be prepared. Why?

Your children will be your largest lasting legacy to this world. They will speak louder on your behalf than any fortune you may amass or any fame you may acquire. They will speak longer, as they will probably outlive you. They will echo everything you did or did not do as a parent. They will reflect the values that you did or did not hold dear. Intelligent people will not be fooled by the eloquent obituary listing your accomplishments; they will simply look at your children to see what kind of person you were.

Your adult children may be taking care of you and making decisions for you as you age. They will treat you with as much consideration and love as you treated them when they were just as vulnerable and perhaps just as helpless. Your reward near the end of your life may be the loving embrace of gratitude or the cool hand of mere obligation, if not neglect. If only for this selfish take on reality, you may want to invest heavily in the well-being of your children.

When you die, you will probably leave all your worldly possessions in the care of your children. If a lifetime's efforts are squandered a few short years after your departure, you will have no one to blame but yourself. If your children have been instilled with rock-solid values and watched a steady, sterling example walk before them (that would be you, old sport), you have a better chance of knowing that your efforts to provide for them, emotionally as well as financially, have not gone unrewarded.

The first part of raising a healthy and happy child begins at conception. The moment a woman realizes she's pregnant, she needs to begin a program of prenatal care with a physician. She also needs to quit drinking alcoholic and caffeinated beverages, stop using drugs, and stop smoking cigarettes. She needs to stop eating junk food and exercise regularly.

The physical and emotional health of your child begins now. If you're too selfish or two undisciplined to not behave in the best interest of your child, don't have a child. Be a selfish and undisciplined adult on your own. No one will blame you for being honest with yourself. You will be blamed, and rightly so, if you bring a child into the world that you don't really want and aren't prepared to take care of. (You should figure this out before you get pregnant.)

The father needs to be on board as well. He'll start reading about the effects pregnancy will have on his wife's body and spirit. He'll pick up some slack with the household responsibilities. He'll be even more considerate of what his wife needs during the next nine months, and he'll realize that he'll have to raise his game during this time. In fact, he's going to have to raise his game for the rest of his life, and the next nine months are just rookie training camp.

Many parents play classical music for and speak and sing to their child during the gestation period. Consider it.

Both parents will receive advice, support, and guidance about the pregnancy, birth, and rearing of their child. Some of it will be sought out. Some of it will come unsolicited. I recommend listening to almost everyone politely, then having long discussions about everything in private. Reach decisions in good time and implement them. If circumstances cause you to reevaluate your choices, sit down and talk about it. If friends and family inquire about why you didn't follow their advice, simply tell them that you decided to make a different choice.

You can decide on how much information you want to share about your decision-making process. If pressed, tell whomever that you've listened to their suggestions, you appreciate their concern, but you and your partner have decided not to do what they've recommended. If they press further, tell them to mind their own business. You can be as blunt as you like, but if their advice turns out to be correct or better in the long run, you need to seek them out and tell them so with the same candor as you dismissed their suggestion earlier. This is great practice for parenting: admitting that you were wrong.

Your child will be born and you'll be delighted. Then, you won't sleep much for the next six to eighteen months and you'll be exhausted. Some simple advice is to sleep when the baby sleeps. Share the feeding and changing responsibilities. And finally, be there.

The most formative years in your child's life are from the time they are born until they're five years old. They will develop the ability to bond emotionally with other human beings (or not) during this time. This will affect the quality, depth, nature, and duration of their relationships they have in childhood, adolescence, and adulthood. Without the ability to bond, they may not be able to empathize, and their behavior may lack awareness or compassion for others.

We watch the news headlines and often wonder how a child can grow up to be a 'monster' and commit horrible crimes. A monster isn't someone who's evil. A monster is someone who doesn't care. You can talk to someone who's evil because they're angry or feel they've suffered an injustice. You can work with that. They might come around. But if someone doesn't care about the impact their behavior has on others, or doesn't realize that their actions actually affect others, you can't reach that and change that because there's nothing there.

Again, this emotional development happens from birth to age five. The human brain develops based on the amount of love it receives during this time. Neglected children don't have the physical brain development that loved children have. The consequences of this are obvious.

You as parents must talk, sing, read, listen to, and hold your child consistently and frequently during this time. Your child has to feel safe as they explore their new world. They should be told frequently that they are special and that they are loved. You should include them in conversations at the dinner table. (This makes the assumption that you're having dinner at the dinner table, not in front of the television.) Talk about things they can relate to. Be aware that they're listening to every word you say. They're watching everything you do. And when it comes down to it, they will ignore what you say and do what you do more often than not.

During this time, you must also introduce your child to books. I did not say you should introduce your child to a smartphone and other electronic devices. I'll tell you now and you'll find out later it's true: smartphones and electronic devices will do your child more harm than good, both intellectually and physically, than anyone will admit right now. The longer your infant child can go without touching a cell phone or a computer, the better off they will be.

Their attention span will be greater. Their ability to relate to others will be better. They will be more literate, more creative, and more human. Trust me on this. They have their entire lives to learn how to operate a computer and be online. Give them the gift of a childhood. Give them the gift of books.

The critical thing that you want to do is to get your child to associate books with love. You do this by reading to them and holding them while you do. You make it a loving, tender time, free from distractions and open to their involvement and their questions. If you have to read the same chapter of the same book for six months because that's what they like, you do it. You take them to a library. You take them to the children's section of the bookstore. Let them meet other young readers. Yes, all this happens before the age of five.

Reading a book engages the mind more than reading online. You want to raise a child who reads and seeks information and wisdom from books and the people who read (and write) books. They will be less inclined to seek solutions to their problems with drugs, alcohol, and sex.

There is a great challenge for this generation of parents: in order to raise your child well, you will probably have to stop looking at your cell phone for a moment. You may not be on social media as much. You may not get all the 'likes' you'd like to get or 'follow' as many people as you'd like because you brought a human being into this world, and they deserve your attention. I know: it's going to be tough.

The first five years, you're going to give your child a lot of love and attention. The second five years, you're going to give them tools, as well. These tools include education and manners. You're going to find the best school you can for them and get them into it. You're going to hire a tutor to come over a couple of nights a week and maybe on the weekend to help them learn a second language or firm up on subjects they're not doing well with. You're going to give them an age-appropriate reading list each summer, in coordination with your local librarian.

They're going to learn the concept of behaving properly in restaurants and at public events. In order to enforce these concepts upon their young minds, you and your partner will learn and perfect the art of *ganging up on your child and being the authority figures in their lives*. You will learn to do the hard, ugly, and unpopular work of disciplining the child you chose to bring into the world.

You are not their friend. You are their parent. You should not care of they 'hate' you for a period of time when you discipline them. You should care if they do not respect you. Some parents say a child should also fear you. They may be right.

If you choose not to discipline and educate your child about how to behave, the world will be a very hard place on them. As casual, trendy, and modern as our social scenes and workplaces seem, they are largely governed by people with manners who hold largely traditional values. If your child is rude and ill-mannered, they're going to have a tough time of it, regardless of how cute you think they are. So do the work now: discipline your child. Teach them that behavior has consequences. If they act out, punish them. If they behave well, compliment them. They want your love. Give it to them unconditionally. They want your approval. Make them earn it. They may dislike the discipline when they're young. They'll thank you for it when they're older.

Your child should learn that they are to dress appropriately. Certain clothing is worn for certain events. They should learn hygiene from you. You may have to learn it yourself first, I don't know. (Wink, nod.) During this time, the concept that the entire world doesn't revolve around your child should occur to your child, and to you. They will realize, with your help, that they are part of a bigger place that was here before they arrived and will be here long after they're gone. So, in some respects, they need to get with the program. Getting a good education, with tutors, and learning how to behave and dress are key parts of this program.

For the following decade, you may be negotiating with your child. As teenagers, they will begin to feel that they are adults. They will want independence, and money to be independent with, if you'd be so kind as to provide that, Dad. They will want to stay out later, go to more places, and associate with people who you may not approve of or don't even know. There's a simple way to handle a lot of this: let the party happen at your house. You won't get as much sleep, but your daughter can stay up as late as she wants with her friends and you can control, to a large extent, what transpires under your roof. It may not be as much fun, of course, but if she wants to hang with *the biker dude*, that's the deal.

You will want to steer your child throughout their young lives. As brilliant, beautiful, and delightful as they may seem to you as their parent, the reality is that many children are just a big bag of bad ideas waiting to come apart at the seams and spill over a cliff. Don't permit that. Your child doesn't know diddly-squat. That's why they have you, their parents.

You will want your child to pursue their own passion, their own career, their own path. However, you want them to maintain the standards of behavior that you have set in your own life. I know a very successful artist who dresses any way he pleases six days a week. However, when his family sits down for dinner on Sunday, he joins them, sporting a blazer, button down shirt, and khakis just like all the other gents at the table.

You'll want to steer them into prioritizing education and attending college. If a child begins at the age of five hearing that they'll attend college because it's just the normal thing to do, they will, in all likelihood, attend college. Their behavior will evolve into accepting that assumption. They really won't seriously consider anything else.

You'll want to steer them into making good manners a habit. You'll do this by setting an example. You'll want to also steer them into dating people who are educated, respectful, and emotionally healthy, and whose families share the same background and values that your family shares. That may sound very Machiavellian, but I happen to think Machiavelli had a lot of good ideas.

A good way to discourage inappropriate suitors and welcome appropriate ones is to establish this rule: the first date your child has with another person will be over dinner with your family at your home. If the young man or young woman is truly interested in your child, then they can sit down to dinner with the family of your child. They will be required to dress appropriately. They will sit at the dinner table without their cell phone. They will engage in conversation with adults, as well as your child.

They will begin the courtship process with the full understanding that they are not just dating your child. They are stepping into your family's world, and they should tread carefully. They can wilt under your ominous gaze or warm in the comfort of shared values and experiences. You can get to know them. They can learn to fear you. It's a good way to establish boundaries and set protocol for the relationship going forward.

You'll want your child to be smart about money. You'll want to give them an allowance and perhaps household responsibilities. At a certain point, let them live on a budget and do without if they run out of money. You'll want them to be aware about money's role in life and what it can and cannot do. You will reinforce the concept that they are not to discuss how much money your family has or how much money anyone else has.

You'll want to steer your child into being smart about sex, alcohol, and drugs. This is best done by constant communication and brutal honesty. Sexually transmitted diseases, unplanned pregnancy, brain damage, and jail time are topics best handled in the open. Remember: communication means listening as well as talking. You'll also want to communicate early and often that you don't give a damn what they're friends are doing or what is popular on social media. You and your spouse are the sole arbiters of what is permitted in your house. This is a great way to say it because your child will, in all likelihood, have to go look up the meaning of 'arbiters'.

If possible, you'll want to take them on vacations, isolated from their peers. This will help you assert positive influence, assess how they're doing, and address any concerns about their behavior in a safe, isolated environment. It also helps reinforce the family bond and reinforce the concept that the family is the priority.

You may want to sit down with your spouse and draft a 'List of Assumptions' for your child prior to them being born. This will take a large number of items off the negotiating table during the teenage years. The List of Assumptions will color your conversations with your child from their infancy until they are an adult. When they see or hear of the bad behavior of some other person and ask you about it, you can simply say, 'That isn't something that we do.'

You want to set your family's standards of behavior above and apart from the behavior of others and reduce the effects of peer pressure from other children. Using the power of the love, attention, communication, and time that you give your child, you make your family the group that asserts the most peer pressure on your child. The family is the unit that your child seeks most of his approval from. They are the people your child least wants to disappoint. The family is your child's primary point of reference.

You may get help from your extended family in steering your child. You may share the List of Assumptions with grandparents, aunts, and uncles. Everyone will be on the same page, and everyone will be telling the child the same thing. The most important thing you can communicate to your child is that they are loved, and that they are very special.

Another one of the most important things you can get your child to assume is that they can accomplish anything they want if they put their mind to it and work for it. You may not believe this, but you can get a child to believe anything. And if a person believes they can do something, or anything, many things in the world are possible for them. I have seen this proven time and time again. And isn't that belief what you want for your child?

Your family will be the 'first sphere of influence' for your child. The 'second sphere of influence' for your child should be the schools they attend. The more rigorous and challenging the academic environment, the more strongly your child will identify with their teachers, fellow students, and their experience. Your child's sense of identity should be as a family member and a student. Following that, they will identify with the group of friends they associate with or a school club or organization they participate in.

For human beings, a sense of belonging is the most important thing in life. Make sure your child has a family unit that gives them that in a loving, supportive sense. Preserve and create traditions that your child can be part of, and not just during holidays.

As your child goes through college and becomes an adult, you will transition from becoming their caretaker and their provider. You may become their friend. You may find it wise at a certain point to stop offering advice unless it is specifically solicited.

You may have to bless or at least accept the marriage of your child to someone you do not approve of. You will have no right to interfere with their relationship unless you suspect abuse. If that occurs, you will contact local law enforcement authorities who handle these situations every day. You will attempt to preserve your relationship with your child by allowing them their dignity under these difficult circumstances. You will be supportive. You will not blame them or allow them to blame themselves if they are the victim of abuse. You will insist they get help if they are the perpetrator.

If, however, your child simply has an argument with their spouse and wants to air the dirty laundry with you, you should decline and tell them to work it out, or not. Do not listen to it. You want to maintain a fair and somewhat distanced, objective opinion of your son or daughter-in-law.

With all the other challenges of raising children — and there are many — I will leave you to resources and professionals more qualified than me.

My final comment being that I believe it's better to be too strict and too traditional than too lenient and too modern.

Questions to Ask and Answer

- Do you really want children? Why?
- Are you prepared emotionally and financially to have a child right now?
- What aspirations do you have for your child?
- Are these fair to them as an individual?
- Or do they simply contribute to the overall quality of life for your child?
- What preparations have you made for your child's healthcare and education?
- Do you have life insurance?
- What things did you parents do for and to you as a child that you want to do for and to your children?
- What things do you want to avoid?
- What habits do you have right now that you wouldn't want your children to have?
- Can you get rid of them or replace them with good habits?
- Were you abused as a child?
- If so, have you discussed this with a qualified professional?
- Do you feel you've addressed and resolved all the issues that come with this trauma?
- Are you willing to make your child the top priority in your life?

In Their Own Words

I came from kind of an upper middle class background. At least that's what I thought until I really started dating David seriously. His family was really wealthy and had been for a really long time, something like a hundred years. We're married now and I don't even know. And, of course, it wasn't something you could tell right away. I thought we were rich because my dad wore a suit and tie to work every day.

"But then the more serious we got, the more I started to see it with David's family. I also sensed the constant assessment that was going on. They knew I didn't have their background. Everyone was polite, but there was a coolness to me from most of his family. I flat out told him after one Christmas with them. He didn't deny it. He just said, 'Yeah. They're waiting to see if you get on board with the way we do things.'

"We had a really big blow out and didn't speak for about a week. I felt really insecure. I felt like David had been really insensitive. We finally talked, and he apologized for what he said, but that that was kind of really what was going on. He told me he loved me and he wanted us to be together, but I had to know that this was the deal. I told him I loved him, too, but he had to back me up against anybody and everybody from now on, even his family. He said he would, and he has.

"For my part, I had to get on board with the Old Money way his family did things. (Yeah, I read your book, and now a lot of their stuff makes sense.) He was completely fine with my mom and dad, so there was no issue there. But I had to brush up on my social skills. Not so much the salad fork and soup spoon details, but just being able to socialize in a world where people didn't talk about money, ever, but where they talked a little about current events, but mostly about ideas they had and what they were doing. And if you weren't doing something interesting or reading a really good book, and couldn't talk about it articulately, God help you at dinner.

"There was also the concept of being dressed all the time, even first thing in the morning. You just didn't come down with bed-head and sweat pants. If I had to use one word for the whole thing, it would be 'rigorous'. But there was energy that came with it, and that is great. Lots of laughter.

"The best part before we got married was when I got a promotion at work. David suggested we meet for dinner at a nice place in town. So I just took off from my office and he told me he'd meet me there. When I got there, I was ready for a candlelit table for two, just me and my man.

"Instead, the waiter takes me back to a private room and I walk in and there's David's whole family, congratulating me. He had called all of them and told them the news. They all left work or whatever and came to the restaurant. They all congratulated me and hugged me and poured me champagne. His sisters were just the best. I just started sniffling after a few minutes. David pulled me aside. I told him they were so sweet. And it was great.

"And that's what's great about them. But if I hadn't made my mind up to up my game and get on board with how they did things, we wouldn't be together. That's kind of my story about marrying someone who's coming from a different social class. One of you is going to have to make a huge effort to fit in.

"I know it's never going to come as easily for me as it does for David's sisters, but I still do it. And I have their total support. It could have been something that drove us apart, but it didn't."

"I was dating this guy and things were going well. We clicked on almost every level. We got to the meet the family stage and my parents loved him. We went to meet his family and I loved them, too. But while we were there, I see him slipping twenty dollar bills to several of his siblings. I mean, not kids, adults.

"So in the car on the way back, I'm asking him about it, and he says, 'Yeah, they're just trying to get it together.' So I'm a little concerned, and the conversation goes on into what happens if we decide to get married, and he's telling me it's not going to change. And he even adds on that when we get a bigger place, if they need a place to stay, they'll probably come and stay with us.

"At that point, I realized it would never work. He couldn't understand. It was just totally normal for him. We went along a little while longer, but there was just no way. I get that you help family out every once in a while, but I don't know if this was a cultural thing or just his siblings taking advantage. I'm really glad I saw it. I'm really glad we talked about it."

"My family was poor growing up. I mean, let's not put any kind of gloss on it. So when I started college, I was working and going to school. I met a girl in my junior year, and we were so in love. I'm still in love with her, in a way. I guess you just never forget that feeling.

"I graduate and she graduates the next year, and we get married. I got a great job at a small firm, plenty of room for growth. Her family was blue collar, too, so I'm thinking, sure, she wants the same things I do, the American dream, do better than your parents, all that.

"I start moving up the ladder and I've got to attend some of the social functions at the local club and at partners' homes and like that. I'm not used to it, but I want to keep making more money, learning more, doing more. And I think that's what she wants, too.

"But she's happy just living like we started out. She's not comfortable getting dressed up and talking with people she doesn't know. It's like pulling teeth to get her to a party. Nobody likes doing some of it, but you do it. That's business.

"I started just going by myself and making excuses for her. Then not even making excuses. Everybody knew. She just didn't fit in. Scratch that. She just didn't want to try. A lot of wives didn't fit in, but they made an effort, so did a few husbands. It's competitive. People above you see the effort and they appreciate it. They reward it. That's the way it is.

"Long story short, we grew apart. She wasn't happy about my hours, even though we had a comfortable life. We weren't in sync with what we were trying to accomplish together. We divorced, I think a year later. It was obvious.

"It broke my heart, but you've got to be with somebody who's maybe got the same background, but for sure has the same ambitions. Otherwise, you're in trouble. We should have talked about that.

"Now, I'm seeing a girl whose uncle works with me, just in another office. She knows the drill, so that part's fine. Early days. We'll see how it goes."

"Advice on marrying someone who doesn't share your religion: My wife and I met in grad school. We have different religious backgrounds, but we'd both traveled a lot and seen a lot. We knew the histories behind our faiths and how some of it was just where you were born, what you were raised doing. God is God. Everybody's just got their own way of worshiping, basically.

"We had a lot of discussions among ourselves and with our sets of parents about getting married. Most of it was how the kids would be raised. My side was more adamant than hers, though everybody finally got the idea that it was going to be our decision, not theirs.

"When we got pregnant and had our first child, everybody was happy. We had the ceremony with my side of the family, then we had her ceremony with her side of the family. Everybody's faith and ritual was acknowledged, and everybody was happy.

"Now the kids are going to school and they're asking 'Am I this or I am this?' We tell them, 'You're both. If you want to choose one day when you're eighteen or twenty-one or whatever, that's up to you.' So they're fine. We live in New York City. Everybody's a mix of something a lot of the time.

"But still, my parents get on a rant about tradition and all that every once in a while. I just have to check them, tell them how it is, and then they're fine. But you better be tough and stand your ground, or the family will try to walk all over you about it."

"You can share what I've written here for your own purposes. You know I support you and your writing. However, you do not have permission to use my name. If you do, I will never speak to you again.

"I think it's a bad idea to marry outside your class. It seldom works. There are just too many assumptions that we make in life. There's no way to communicate them all to someone who doesn't share them. You can adopt values and even manners, and I applaud people who do. It is truly essential to upward mobility. More importantly, they elevate your quality of life, a concept that is not as understood or appreciated as it could be.

"However, there are limits to what one can do without losing one's identity. My grandchildren refer to it as being a 'poser.' By that I believe they mean 'impostor'. I met the child to whom they were referring. He just wants to be accepted. No, he's not one of us, but that shouldn't stop them from being friends. I have all sorts of friends. It makes life interesting, and it keeps you from getting a fat head. Act like a prima ballerina and your real friends will take you down a peg in a second, especially the ones who don't care what country club you belong to.

"Marriage is about compatibility. If you have shared experiences and shared expectations, you're half the way there. Love does not conquer all. Daily life conquers all. You should be in the fight with someone who understands your world without a second thought. Most often, that comes from marrying someone who has the same background.

"This may sound elitist. I've been called worse. When you have something of value to preserve and protect, you do get selective about the people you let in. The old families, and even the newly rich ones, are very particular about who their children see. The French old guard have their *rallyes*. We have clubs. At college, we have fraternities and sororities. These serve the function of steering the younger ones to those with whom they have the most in common.

"We have money, of course. We also have a position within the community. For a newcomer, that's not an easy transition to make. You can't just do what you please because you have money. Most of the time, it's not that the new ones lack intelligence. It's that they lack restraint. That's a difficult thing to teach.

"Off topic, I'm very happy the gay community can marry now. I think it's going to increase stability in society. Young people will see more commitment all around. Perhaps they'll enter into relationships with a little more thought. Perhaps we can leave the world with a little less prejudice and a little more love."

In Summary

When two people marry, no one really knows what's going to happen. That's the truth, no matter what advice anyone gives you. It's a gamble, but if you consider and implement the concepts and practices I've detailed in this book, you might be able to moderate the risk. You will certainly be able to identify some issues and perhaps construct and implement some solutions that will help you and your partner have a successful marriage or avoid a painful mistake. My hope, above all, is that you will find love and be happy.

I believe in the institution of marriage, as challenging as it is sometimes. We have developed a fetish for innovation lately. We bow down to the gods of technology and rarely stand our ground and face the winds of change. Change is sometimes progress, sometimes not. In the midst of all this information at our fingertips, we'd be wise not to lose sight with the sacred traditions in our past. They have become permanent and remained important for good reason. They have a purpose and they have value. Marriage is one of those key sacred traditions. Learning how to do it well is a worthwhile pursuit, and it is especially helpful to learn about it prior to getting into it.

I think the key to happiness is contradictory: we find happiness for ourselves when we give our love to someone else, when we make them the priority in our lives, and when the feeling and commitment is mutual. I think that structure is important in people's lives and that marriage is a part of that structure. Some of history's greatest poetry was created when the literary mores of the day dictated a certain structure for meter and rhyme. I think the same discipline and structure benefits relationships, helping them to rise to joyful heights.

I think it's best to enter into marriage with your heart and your head. It's just too big of a commitment and too long a road to think that romance alone is going to carry the day. That said, there is no substitute for the magic that happens between two people. I enjoy it every day, and I feel like the luckiest man on the planet. You may see this as yet another contradiction. Perhaps it is.

When it's all said and done, you probably need 'the strategy' and 'the magic' to make a marriage work for a lifetime. I'm the person who's tried to articulate the strategy in this book. It's up to you to find the person who, for you, makes the magic.

I wish you every success.

Newlyweds - Bobea and Jean-Pierre Taieb

About the Author

Byron Tully is the author of *The Old Money Book*; *Old Money, New Woman: How To Manage Your Money and Your Life*; and *Old Money Style: Secrets To Dressing Well For Less - Gentleman's Edition*.

After turning down a full scholarship to Brown University, Byron Tully moved to Los Angeles and began writing for the entertainment industry. In 2013, he penned *The Old Money Book*.

As well as authoring the 'Old Money' series of books, Byron curates The Old Money Book blog (www.theoldmoneybook.com), which has been visited by over 1 million readers worldwide.

He lives in Europe with his wife, an Old Money Gal from Boston.

www.ingramcontent.com/pod-product-compliance
Lightning Source LLC
Chambersburg PA
CBHW072016110526
44592CB00012B/1329